RebuildingBooks
For Divorce and Beyond

WORKBOOK FOR

REBUILDING

SECOND EDITION

When Your Relationship Ends

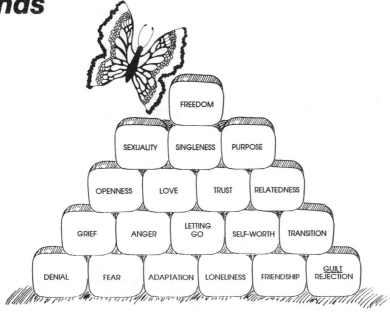

FREEDOM

SEXUALITY · SINGLENESS · PURPOSE

OPENNESS · LOVE · TRUST · RELATEDNESS

GRIEF · ANGER · LETTING GO · SELF-WORTH · TRANSITION

DENIAL · FEAR · ADAPTATION · LONELINESS · FRIENDSHIP · GUILT REJECTION

BRUCE FISHER, Ed.D.

WITH JERE BIERHAUS

Impact ❧ Publishers,® Inc.
ATASCADERO, CALIFORNIA 93423-6016

Publisher's Note
This publication is designed to provide accurate and authoritative information in regard to the subject matter covered. It is sold with the understanding that the publisher is not engaged in rendering psychological, medical, or other professional services. If expert assistance or counseling is needed, the services of a competent professional should be sought.

Acknowledgments:
Session opening illustrations by Sharon Wood Schnare, San Luis Obispo, California
Other illustrations by Margaret Raab, Denver, Colorado
Some material in this workbook was provided by Jere Bierhaus of Denver, Colorado, who has been teaching the Ten-Week Rebuilding Seminar since 1991.

Permissions:
"The Johari Window," on page 56 from *Group Process: An Introduction to Group Dynamics,* Third Edition, by Joseph Luft, Copyright © 1984, 1970, 1963 by Joseph Luft. Reprinted by permission of Mayfield Publishing Company.

"101 Ways to Praise a Child," on page 16 reprinted with permission from The Bureau for At-Risk Youth, 1-800-99-YOUTH

"Social Readjustment Rating Scale," on page 22 by Holmes, Thomas H. and Rahe, Richard H. "The Social Readjustment Rating Scale," Journal of Psychosomatic Research, Vol. II, No. 2, August, 1967, pp. 213-218.

"So What Can I Do About My Anger?" on pages 36-37 and "Effective Listening" on page 74 from *Your Perfect Right,* 7th Edition, by Robert E. Alberti and Michael L. Emmons© 1995. Reprinted by permission of Impact Publishers, Inc.

Please Note:
Some of the material in this *Workbook* has been "borrowed from other sources." Permission has been acquired from the copyright owner for those items whose source is known. If you are the author, or you know the author, of an item marked "author unknown," please notify Impact Publishers, Inc. We want to give credit where credit is due.

Impact Publishers and colophon are registered trademarks of Impact Publishers, Inc.
Printed in the United States of America on acid-free paper.
Published by **Impact ✍ Publishers®, Inc.**
POST OFFICE BOX 6016
ATASCADERO, CALIFORNIA 93423-6016
www.impactpublishers.com

Contents

How to Use This Workbook v

Welcome to The Fisher Seminar vi

Participant's Registration Agreement vii

Personal Information Sheet viii

Outline and Overview of The Ten Sessions ix

Introduction to the Second Edition x

The Ten Sessions

   Session One — *The Rebuilding Blocks* Lesson Plan 1

      Notes on "The Rebuilding Blocks" 2

      "I Am Female and My Life is in Shambles!" 3

      "I Am Male and I Am Totally Alone" 4

      Affirmations 5

      Journaling Page 6

   Session Two — *Adaptation* Lesson Plan 9

      Adaptive Behavior Homework Sheet 10

      Page for Presentation Notes 11

      List of Adaptive Behaviors 12

      Authentic and Adaptive/Survivor Behaviors 13

      It Is Never My Responsibility... 14

      Words of Wisdom to "Rescuers" 15

      "101 Ways to Praise a Child" 16

      Risks. A Hug is a Great Gift. 17

      Affirmations 18

      Journaling Page 19

   Session Three — *Grief* Lesson Plan 21

      Life Stress and Physical Illness 22

      Page for Presentation Notes 23

      Letting Go 24

      Then, Now, and Tomorrow 25

      Good-bye Letters 26

      Affirmations 29

   Session Four — *Anger* Lesson Plan 31

      Healthy Ways to Work On Anger 32

      Page for Presentation Notes 33

      Illustrating Relationships with Body Sculpturing 34

      So What Can I Do About My Anger? 36

      Relationships Are My Teachers. The Swing. 38

      Affirmations 39

   Session Five — *Self-Worth* Lesson Plan 41

      Steps to Improving Your Feelings of Self-Worth 42

      Page for Presentation Notes 43

      Rules for Being Human 44

      I'm Okay — You're Okay. Hugging. 45

      Affirmations 46

      Journaling Page 47

Session Six — *Transition* **Lesson Plan**   49
    Fisher's Theory of Growth and Development   50
    Page for Presentation Notes   51
    Affirmations   52
    Journaling Page   53

Session Seven — *Openness* **Lesson Plan**   55
    Johari Window   56
    Page for Presentation Notes   57
    Please Hear What I Am Not Saying   58
    I Am Me. Small Group Activity.   59
    Affirmations   60
    Journaling Page   61

Session Eight — *Love* **Lesson Plan**   63
    What Do You Know About Love?   64
    Page for Presentation Notes   65
    Love   66
    Happiness — It's Only Natural   67
    Affirmations   68
    Journaling Page   69

Session Nine — *Relatedness* **Lesson Plan**   71
    Today. Growing Relationships.   72
    Page for Presentation Notes   73
    Listening is Loving. Effective Listening. Attending Skills.   74
    Questions for Discussion   75
    Affirmations   76
    Journaling Page   77

Session Ten — *Sexuality* **Lesson Plan**   79
    Sexuality Questionnaire   80
    Page for Presentation Notes   81
    Affirmations   82
    Journaling Page   83

Appendix A
    Fisher Divorce Adjustment Scale and Answer Sheet   85

Appendix B
    Rebuilding Seminar Final Course Evaluation   89

Appendix C
    Rebuilding Blocks for Widows & Orphans   91
    Fisher Widowed and Widowers Adjustment Scale and Answer Sheet   98

Appendix D
    Welcome Volunteer Helpers   103
    Volunteer Helper Agreement   104
    Volunteer Helper's Duties   105
    Volunteer Special Assignment Sheet   106
    Specific Suggestions for Volunteer Helpers   107
    Fisher Volunteer Assessment Scale   110

How To Use This Workbook

Rebuilding after a crisis is a do-it-yourself project. This workbook is designed to be used with the book *Rebuilding: When Your Relationship Ends"* in the ten-week educational program known as the "Fisher Rebuilding Seminar." Readers who have thought about writing in the *Rebuilding* book now have this workbook to write in. We believe using this workbook will enhance your growth and assist you in your adjustment process while participating in the ten-week class. If you are reading the book and not participating in the seminar, we think you'll find the workbook helpful.

The Ten Selected Chapters in *Rebuilding*

We have identified what we believe to be the most important and difficult to understand chapters in *Rebuilding* to study during the ten weeks of the Rebuilding Seminar. The lesson plans suggest reading the rest of the chapters in *Rebuilding* when you have time. You may want to read the complete book as you begin the seminar, and then spend extra time each week reading the chapter that will be emphasized in the next session of the seminar. You may find the "How Are You Doing?" checklist at the end of each chapter good discussion questions. After the ten-week seminar is completed, we suggest that you go back and finish any homework you were not able to do during the Seminar. You may find it helpful to do some of the homework exercises again.

Volunteer Helpers

We have included a section in this workbook (Appendix D) for volunteer helpers. Volunteer helpers are graduates of the ten-week seminar who are invited to come back and be active listeners and helpers to the present class participants. We believe volunteers will enjoy using the same workbook as you go through the class again as a volunteer helper.

Confidentiality

We want you to think about confidentiality as you write in this workbook. You may want to keep a separate and more personal journal in addition to this book. We suggest you write your name in this book so it will easily be identified as your book.

Widows and Widowers

The majority of people reading *Rebuilding* and participating in the Rebuilding Seminar are ending a relationship through divorce, but we know that some readers and participants may be widows or widowers. This workbook includes a modified version of the first chapter in *Rebuilding*, and a modified version of the *Fisher Divorce Adjustment Scale* for widowed people. (See Appendix C.) We hope these two additions will make the class more helpful for widowed people.

We hope you will find this workbook helpful as you work through the process of Rebuilding after a crisis in your life.

Welcome to the
Fisher "Rebuilding When Your Relationship Ends" Seminar

We want to welcome you and to acknowledge you for finding the courage to enroll in the ten-week seminar. The seminar has been offered all over the planet — more than a quarter of a million people have participated.

This is an *educational seminar*, including a textbook, homework assignments, a structured format for each session described in the lesson plans and specific behavioral objectives. This is not intended to be a *group therapy* experience, which is much less structured and has different objectives and goals. This educational model is proven to be a highly effective method to help people adjust to the ending of a love relationship.

The seminar is designed to help you make your crisis — the ending of your love relationship — into a creative experience. A crisis usually includes emotional and psychological pain. If this pain can be embraced and used as motivation to grow and adjust, it can also help you learn to take charge of your life. Most graduates of this seminar are better able to recover from the ending of their love relationship, and they are also more capable of building and creating lasting and healthy relationships in the future.

Supplementing the lectures and group activities in the class are the following components of the Rebuilding Seminar.

Rebuilding: When Your Relationship Ends, Third Edition (2000)

The textbook uses the Rebuilding Blocks concept to help people understand the adjustment process of rebuilding after a crisis. There are twenty chapters in the textbook. Ten of them will be assigned during the seminar. The appendix includes, "Kids Are Tougher Than You Think: The Rebuilding Blocks Process for Kids," and introduces the concept of "The Healing Separation" — an alternative to divorce.

Rebuilding Workbook

This workbook is to be used in conjunction with the book for those attending the Rebuilding Seminar. It has been designed to guide participants through the ten sessions of the seminar. It also provides space to take notes and write feelings and reactions to the seminar experience and reading assignments. It includes supplemental information not found in the textbook. It is an essential part of the seminar, and is also a very helpful resource for those who are working through this difficult life crisis on their own.

Facilitator's Manual

The *Facilitator's Manual* provides information for leaders of the seminar. Part 1 includes the Lesson Plans which describe and discuss the format for each of the ten sessions. Part 2 is designed to answer questions the facilitator might have while teaching the seminar. Part 3 describes the use of the *Fisher Divorce Adjustment Scale*. Part 4 describes the Volunteer Helper Program.

Fisher Divorce Adjustment Scale

This is a 100-item personal adjustment scale designed to give you feedback about how well you're handling the ending of your love relationship. It will be used as a pre-test in the seminar to help you understand the areas you need to work on. It also will be given as a post-test to give you feedback about the growth you experienced during the ten weeks of the seminar.

Volunteer Helpers Support Program

Upon completing the ten-week seminar, certain graduates may be selected and asked to be volunteer helpers in a later seminar. There is a training session to prepare them to be better volunteers. They take part in the seminar each week by leading small group discussions, giving support to others, and assisting the facilitator in various ways. They also arrange and attend various social gatherings outside the seminar. Their most important function is to give support to the participants, especially by calling them in between the sessions of the seminar. The volunteers are an important part of the seminar, but they are not trained facilitators.

Participant's Registration Agreement
for the
Rebuilding Seminar

The Rebuilding Seminar is a ten-week educational program designed to help people adjust to the ending of a love relationship. It is not a therapy group. The seminar meets for three hours, one night a week for ten weeks, a total of thirty contact hours. In order to receive the maximum benefit from this seminar, you are encouraged to attend as many of the ten sessions as possible, and to complete as much of the homework as possible.

The textbook for this seminar is the third edition of the best-selling book *Rebuilding: When Your Relationship Ends*. In addition, each participant will be provided with the *Rebuilding Workbook*. The facilitator may include the cost of these two books in the fee for the seminar, or you may be asked to purchase them separately.

Registration Agreement:

I understand that I will experience more growth during this class if I attend all ten sessions, and do the assigned homework. I agree to do both to the best of my ability.

I agree that information of a personal nature which is shared with me by a participant, volunteer, or facilitator involved in this seminar will be kept strictly confidential by me during and after this seminar.

I understand that I may benefit from the friendship and support of other people involved in this seminar. I acknowledge it could be detrimental to everyone involved if, during this seminar, I enter into romantic or sexual relationships with others. I agree to not become romantically or sexually involved with other seminar participants, volunteers, or facilitators during this ten week seminar.

I understand that this is a supportive educational seminar and not a therapy group. I specifically release the facilitators involved in this seminar from any responsibility for my wellness. I unconditionally release them from all liability whatsoever as a result of my interaction with other seminar participants, volunteers, or facilitators during the duration of this seminar and at any time in the future. I agree to be accountable and responsible for my own behavior.

Fee:

The fee for this ten-week seminar is $_____. A minimum of $ _____ is due by opening night as a non-refundable registration fee. I have paid $_____ before or on opening night. I agree to pay the remainder of the fee no later than the sixth night of the seminar. I will receive a $_____ discount if I previously purchased the textbook. There will be no refund of fees paid under any circumstances unless agreed to in writing by the facilitator.

I have read and completely understand and agree to the terms of this agreement. I further understand that failure to comply with any of the terms of this agreement may result in my being terminated from participation in this educational seminar.

_____

Name

_____

Address   City   Zip

_____   _____

Home Phone   Work Phone

_____   _____   _____

Signature of seminar participant   Signature of seminar facilitator   Date

Both the participant and the facilitator should retain a copy of this sheet.

Personal Information Sheet for the Rebuilding Seminar

Please answer the following questions. (All information will be kept confidential)

Name _____ Home phone _____

Address _____ Work phone _____

City, State _____ Zip _____ Birthday _____

Relationship Situation:
Who ended your last relationship? ____You did ✔Your former love-partner did ____You both did

____ Single ____ Separated ____ Divorced ____ Married ____ Widowed

____ Not dating ____ Casual dating ____ Dating one person only ____ Living together ✔ Engaged

Separated _2_ months. Married ____ years.

Employment:
Name of
employer_____Occupation_____

____ Work with others ____ Work alone ____ Involved in management

Children:
Ages _____ When do they spend time with you? _____

Family of Origin and Childhood Experiences: ____ Basically happy, normal childhood
✔ Parents divorced ____ Parent(s) alcoholic ✔ Parent(s) died ____ Parents' marriage unhappy
✔ Childhood verbal abuse ✔ Childhood physical abuse ✔ Childhood sexual abuse
____ Adopted _10_ Birth Order _4_ # of sisters _2_ # of brothers

Therapy Situation:
Are you presently seeing a therapist for individual ~~or marital~~ counseling? ✔yes __ no
If yes, have you discussed attending this seminar with your therapist? __ yes ✔no
Therapist's Name _____ Therapist's Phone Number_____

How did you hear about this Seminar?
___ Friend who had taken seminar   ___ Attorney   ___ Clergy person
___ Counselor or therapist   ___ Newspaper   ___ Doctor
___ Read one of Bruce's books   ___ TV or Radio Show   ✔ Other-explain: _support group._

Goals and reasons for taking this seminar.
1.
2.
3.
4.
5.

Facilitators: We suggest you make a copy of this sheet and retain the copy in your files.

Outline and Overview of the Ten Sessions
for the
Rebuilding Seminar

The following is an overview of the ten sessions of the seminar and the topics to be discussed in each session. The reading assignments listed are chapters from the book *Rebuilding: When Your Relationship Ends,* third edition, by Dr. Bruce Fisher and Dr. Robert Alberti. Notice that some of the chapters in the book are not covered in these ten sessions. We have identified the topics which are typically the most important and challenging, and we believe you will benefit the most by covering them during the seminar. If you have the time and energy you will find it helpful to read the chapters in the book which are not emphasized in the ten-week seminar. We encourage you to keep meeting as a group, discussing each of the remaining chapters after the ten-week seminar is completed.

Session One: **The Rebuilding Blocks.** Chapter 1, pages 5-28. The rebuilding blocks give you an overview of the adjustment process used in this seminar to help you make your crisis into a creative experience.

Session Two: **Adaptation** - "But it Worked When I Was a Kid." Chapter 4, pages 52-65. You may have learned and developed adaptive behavior during your formative years in order to get your needs met. This adaptive behavior may become maladaptive behavior in your adult relationships. You may find it helpful to develop more authentic behavior.

Session Three: **Grief -** "There's This Terrible Feeling of Loss." Chapter 8, pages 96-109. An important aspect of ending a love relationship is grieving your various losses of love. There is a connection between overcoming denial, grieving, and disentangling from the former love partner.

Session Four: **Anger -** "Damn the S.O.B.!" Chapter 9, pages 110-127. Ending a love relationship results in feelings of anger. Resolving this anger allows you to find forgiveness for yourself and for your former love partner. It is important to deal with your angry feelings because they can last for months and maybe years after the physical separation.

Session Five: **Self-worth -** "Maybe I'm Not So Bad After All." Chapter 11, pages 136-146. The previous sessions have helped you work through your painful feelings. Improving your feelings of self-worth will help you move beyond pain and find the strength to grow.

Session Six: **Transition -** "I'm Waking Up and Putting Away My Leftovers." Chapter 12, pages 148-164. After improving your self-worth, you are emotionally stronger and ready to experience personal growth. You are ready to wake up and begin taking charge of your life.

Session Seven: **Openness –** "I've Been Hiding Behind A Mask." Chapter 13, pages 166-175. You have been using a great deal of emotional energy trying to be someone other than who really you are. You may choose to be free to be you.

Session Eight: **Love -** "Could Somebody Really Care for Me?" Chapter 14, pages 176-187. It is okay to love yourself. The more you love yourself, the more authentically you can love others.

Session Nine: **Relatedness -** "Growing Relationships Help Me Rebuild." Chapter 16, pages 200-215. The relationships that develop following the ending of an important relationship can be an important part of your growing process. You may find the friendships you make in this class help you to grow and adjust.

Session Ten: **Sexuality -** "I'm Interested, but I'm Scared." Chapter 17, pages 216-232. You long for emotional intimacy but you're afraid. Intimacy starts with becoming better acquainted and more intimate with yourself. Understanding your own sexuality, and learning more about the way others feel will be very helpful.

Introduction to the Second Edition

You've signed up for the ten-week Fisher Rebuilding Seminar? Congratulations! You're in for a life-changing experience. *Approximately 80% of the graduates of the ten-week class have developed a successful love relationship after completing the class,* according to Bruce Fisher's research. Many others have gone back to work on previous relationships that they thought were ending.

Or perhaps you're reading this workbook because you've read *Rebuilding: When Your Relationship Ends,* and you're looking for help in applying its ideas in your life. You'll find the ten-week lesson plans a very helpful structure for working through your divorce recovery process. (Of course, you'll miss the valuable group support enjoyed by those who participate in the seminar.)

The *Rebuilding Workbook* has evolved as the best blueprint of structured help for those who want to continue their work in rebuilding their lives after the ending of a love relationship. Over the years when Bruce conducted the Rebuilding Seminar classes, he regularly presented a questionnaire, asking participants what they thought was important to learn in the sessions. This workbook is the result of over two decades of experience in refining the seminar, based on expert feedback from those who have gone through the process.

One of the main insights that participants gain from the class is that *both partners contribute to the ending of a relationship.* Many people have discovered that they've harbored unresolved issues within themselves, and have projected those issues onto their partners — a major cause of unhappiness and emotional pain. The class helps foster self-knowledge and internal healing of those issues, allowing the creation of healthy new relationships — or sometimes even a renewed relationship with the old partner.

Those who take part in the Fisher Rebuilding Seminar often take longer to become involved in another committed relationship. That waiting period increases the chances of creating a more healing and happier love relationship, with a far better chance of survival. Insights gained through the classes often improve relationships with members of the family and friends as well as love partners, thus broadly enhancing and enriching the quality of life.

Taking the class — or working your way through this *Workbook* on your own — is time well spent. The work involved should result in a new confidence in yourself and your ability to handle the ups and downs that are the inevitable part of every life.

Bruce Fisher's work has touched hundreds of thousands — perhaps millions — of lives. An estimated half-million people have participated in the ten-week Rebuilding class — in the U.S., Canada, England, Australia, Sweden, Finland, and elsewhere. Three-quarters of a million copies of *Rebuilding: When Your Relationship Ends* were in print at the turn of the 21st century. Word of mouth has accounted for the tremendous popularity of the "Rebuilding Block" system because this process *works*. It has helped countless lives to mend after the shattering experience of divorce, and one friend tells another.

Before Bruce left us in 1998, he prepared a clear statement of his ideas for improvement of this workbook. This second edition reflects his desired changes, corresponds to the third (2000) edition of *Rebuilding: When Your Relationship Ends*, and brings the material up to date for the 21st century. Reader comments and suggestions are always welcome to help us improve future editions. That's the way Bruce wanted it.

— Robert E. Alberti, Ph.D., Editor
Co-author, *Rebuilding: When Your Relationship Ends*

Session One
The Rebuilding Blocks

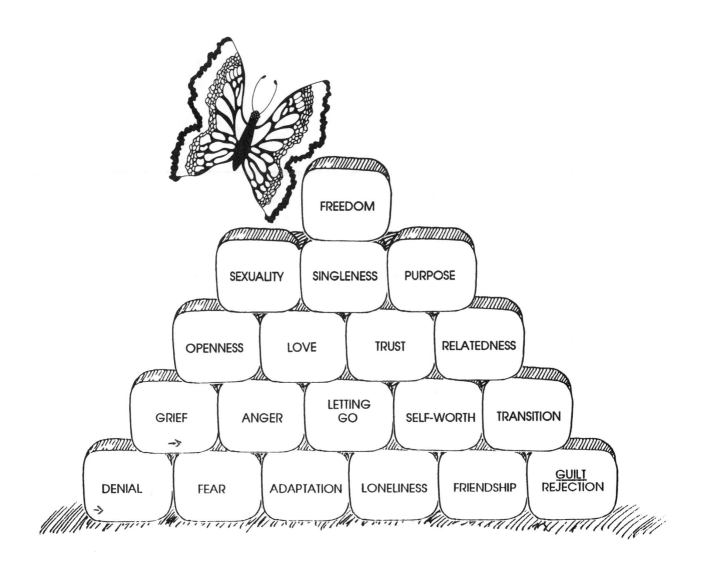

FREEDOM

SEXUALITY   SINGLENESS   PURPOSE

OPENNESS   LOVE   TRUST   RELATEDNESS

GRIEF   ANGER   LETTING GO   SELF-WORTH   TRANSITION

DENIAL   FEAR   ADAPTATION   LONELINESS   FRIENDSHIP   GUILT REJECTION

You are probably experiencing the painful feelings that come when a love relationship ends. There is a proven 19-step process of adjustment to the loss of a love. This session provides an overview and an introduction to the Rebuilding Blocks which form that process.

Lesson Plan for Session One

The Rebuilding Blocks

Goals for Session One:
1. To recognize that rebuilding your life when a love relationship ends is a process that takes time.
2. To understand how the Rebuilding process — as pictured by the Rebuilding Blocks — will help.
3. To get to know the other seminar participants, the volunteer(s), and the leader(s).
4. To commit to confidentiality: anything personal shared here, stays here.
5. To understand the importance of three key tools for your learning and growth process: homework; a journal; affirmations.

Agenda for Session One (assumes an evening meeting time):

6:30 to 7:00 p.m. Sign in at the door, put on a name tag, help yourself to something to drink, get acquainted with other participants and volunteer helpers, and make yourself comfortable.

7:00 to 8:30 p.m. Presentation about Dr. Bruce Fisher's "Rebuilding Blocks" by the facilitator(s).

(This presentation is open to the public.)
8:30 to 9:00 p.m. Break
1. Register for the seminar by filling out a registration agreement and turning it in with a check to a facilitator.
2. Pick up copies of *Rebuilding: When Your Relationship Ends*, and the *Rebuilding Workbook*.
3. Sign your name to the "Class Attendance Sheet." Mark H on the week you would like the class to meet in your home and G on the week you would like to bring goodies.

(Registered participants *only* after break)
9:00 to 9:10 p.m. Pass out class lists. Discuss the homework assignments, journaling, affirmations.

9:10 to 9:50 p.m. Small groups, led by volunteer helpers. Sample questions:
- Which "Rebuilding Blocks" appear to be the most challenging for you?
- What is your present relationship situation?
- Tell us something about yourself so we can get to know you better.
- What do you hope to get out of this seminar?

9:50 to 10:00 p.m. Big group time and closure.

Homework For Next Week's Seminar: (* Indicates Most Important Homework)
*1. Take the "Fisher Divorce Adjustment Scale" and bring back the completed answer sheet next week.
*2. Read Chapter 4, "Adaptation" in *Rebuilding: When Your Relationship Ends*.
*3. Call three people in the class in order to start building a support system. Use the small group sample questions on tonight's lesson plan as a guideline for something to talk about.
*4. Fill out the personal information sheet and turn it in to a facilitator next week.
 5. Read Chapter 1, "The Rebuilding Blocks" in the book to review the presentation of Session One.
 6. Start keeping a journal. Write as many "I feel _____" messages as possible. You may wish to start by writing your reactions to opening night after class tonight.
 7. If possible, read chapters 2 and 3 in the book.
 8. If you can't make it to the seminar one night, please call your facilitator. Thanks!

Notes on "The Rebuilding Blocks"

			Freedom			
		Sexuality	Singleness	Purpose		
	Openness	Love	Trust	Relatedness	
Grief	Anger	Letting Go	Self Worth	Transition
Denial	Fear	Adaptation	Loneliness	Friendship	Guilt/Rejection

Please write your reactions to the Rebuilding Block Presentation

1. **Denial**

2. **Fear**

3. **Adaptation**

4. **Loneliness**

5. **Friendship**

6. **Guilt/Rejection**

7. **Grief**

8. **Anger**

9. **Letting Go**

10. **Self-Worth**

11. **Transition**

12. **Openness**

13. **Love**

14. **Trust**

15. **Relatedness**

16. **Sexuality**

17. **Singleness**

18. **Purpose**

19. **Freedom**

I Am Female And My Life Is In Shambles!

(To be read by all human beings)

Just as the last few pieces of the picture puzzle of who am I were being put in place,
Someone came along and knocked all of the pieces on the floor.
What do I do?—my life is in shambles.

I have never felt so confused and crazy.
How can I go on?
Who am I?
If I don't know who I am, how can I continue to work? to parent? to face my friends? to convince my parents
they aren't a failure because of my divorce?

I am the one who is responsible for the members of my family.
I took on that job at some time—I don't know when.
But I do know I failed at what a woman is supposed to be—the one who holds the family together.

The pieces of me seem to be so chaotic that I will never be able to sort them out,
I thought I knew the colors and shapes of the various parts of me.
Now I question how I could have been so dumb, so naive, so false and inauthentic.
I want to hide and not let anyone know what a mess I am.

Wow! I got the courage to come to opening night of the Rebuilding class,
Thank you Jane for talking me into coming.
I wanted to be here but be invisible so no one can see my pain.
I was surprised to find others who appeared to be in as much pain as me.
I decided I was not so all alone.

I watched the Rebuilding blocks fit together,
I even climbed some of the mountain internally and began to feel some hope.
Can I trust the Rebuilding blocks?
Will the process work for me?
It has worked for thousands of others
What have I got to lose?
There is nothing deeper and more frightening than the abyss I have been in since I separated.
I might as well give it a try. Sign me up for the climb up the mountain.

Embrace my Pain? Are you kidding?
I would much sooner embrace another warm body.
But even that thought is scary.
Anything I think about doing is scary.
"Your pain is the breaking of the shell of your understanding,
It is the bitter potion by which the Physician within you heals your sick self."
I want to heal. I want to become. I want to be happy and free—more than I have ever been.
Embracing my pain is not what I thought I would be doing when I decided to become married.

I want to tell my story. Tell everyone how unfair it is. To feel sorry for myself.
It made sense when I heard that it was okay to talk out whatever I was feeling.
And to say at the end of my story—"But I am working on it" was a new idea.
I do think it is my story and not anyone else's.
Maybe I can create the ending of my story and make it turn out like I want it to.

Thank you Jane for helping me be here tonight.
I am committed to climb to the top of the mountain and find freedom.
I will put the pieces together and find my identity.
I will take charge of my life and become the person I am capable of being.
I am committed to grow. I am committed to be me.

I Am Male And I Am Totally Alone

(To be read by all human beings)

I was sitting by the warm fire of married love,
Suddenly I am alone and out in the cold.
It's not so bad. I can adjust to anything because I am a strong and self sufficient male.
Why do I feel so cold?

I provided like my father did.
My family never went hungry.
I want someone to hug me—but my father never did.
The most warmth I have ever known is when she loved me.
And now I don't feel her love anymore.

I kept busy—maybe too busy to feel.
It is so cold out here. I want to find warm love again.
I didn't know I could be so lonely.
The emptiness inside of me is absolute.
I think I have been vacuum packed inside of a shell that it impermeable.

John told me about this class.
Said there would be other males here who were just as lonely as I.
I told him I was the only person on the North Pole and there was no one else like me.
I am beginning to discover I was wrong.
I never thought I could be wrong. Males are always right. My father taught me that.

Wow! The Rebuilding blocks make so much sense.
Climbing the mountain looks like an adventure—a problem I can solve.
It is scary to have to climb alone. She used to hold my hand when I felt afraid.
Maybe the textbook will be a trail guide for me to help me find my way alone.
It seems to be the only friend I have right now.
The book helps me to understand what I am experiencing.
No one ever helped me to understand myself before.
This climb is scary because I have to feel instead of keeping busy.
Where is my mommy?

Embrace my pain? Grieve? Us males don't grieve. That's only for females.
But I am cold. What can I do to feel warmer? How can I keep from freezing to death?
I become uncomfortable when I feel. Surprise! I'm not as cold when I am uncomfortable.
Maybe the coldness I feel is within me.
Maybe it is not because she is gone but because I am gone. Gone from myself.
Maybe I can create a warm fire of love within me. Something that will keep the cold away.

I've decided I need to climb the mountain.
It is a new and different journey—not like what I learned about life from father.
What did I learn about life from him? I never knew him.
Maybe I learned loneliness from him. I never thought about him being lonely till now.
Sign me up. I need this class. Maybe I need to learn that males grieve also.

I see myself as hard with her providing softness to my life.
I see myself needing her in order to feel for me when I couldn't feel for me.
I want to find softness within me to balance out my hardness.
I want to become whole, more balanced, warm inside.

I don't want to say "But I'm working on it."
I just want to learn how to tell my story like my female friends do so easily.
I want my life to unfold gently like a flower blooming,
Instead of my life being the solution to a math problem.
I am committed to grow. I am committed to be me.

Affirmations

Writing and saying affirmations out loud can be a powerful experience. Here are some examples of affirmations. We invite you to write one or more affirmations that are important for you in your own personal growth and self-actualization. Post them in a prominent place and say them out loud at least once a day.

1. I am making this crisis into a creative experience.
2. I am learning new and healthier ways of interacting with others.
3. I am taking charge of my life and creating the happiness I deserve.

My first affirmation is:

I will recover for this and I will be stronger

My second affirmation is:

I will learn and not allow myself to be hurt again!

My third affirmation is:

I will learn to trust my guts instinct.

My reactions to the reading assignment in *Rebuilding* are:

How long will it takes for me to recover & be happy again?

My reactions to the first session of the Rebuilding class are:

There is hope.

What were some of the important things I learned in Session One?

Recovery takes time
I must grieve or let go before I can be healed

What are some of the important changes I am making in my thinking and my actions?

thinking — write my thoughts & Counter them

Actions: No NC

Journal

We suggest you keep a journal while participating in this ten-week class. It is helpful to start each sentence in your journal with the pronoun "I." "I feel" messages are even more helpful. You may find it helpful to write in your journal after each night of the class. We suggest you write daily. Find the frequency of writing that works best for you. These pages are provided for you to use for your first entry. We suggest you obtain a small notebook for your ongoing journal.

12-29-04

I feel sick in my stomach when I think of how I was being used or tossed.

I feel sick at the way one person treats another.

I feel sick when someone said "I love you" & don't really mean it.

I feel sick @ my own impulsive behaviors.

Session Two
Adaptation
"But It Worked When I Was a Kid!"

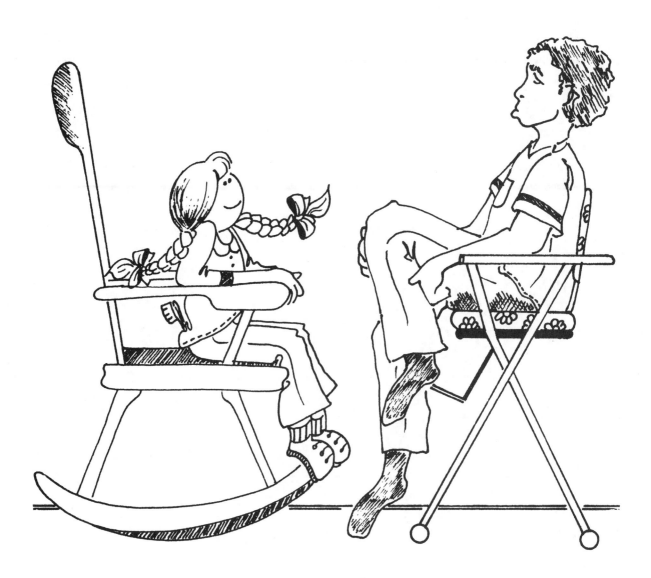

Growing up, we all learned a variety of ways to adapt when our needs for love and attention were unfulfilled. Some of those strategies may have helped us get by as children, but they are excess baggage for grown-ups. An over- or under-responsible style, for example, is not effective in adult relationships. The process of rebuilding offers many opportunities to change your unhealthy parts into authentic, relationship-enhancing behaviors.

Lesson Plan for Session Two

Adaptation: But It Worked When I Was a Kid!

Goals for Session Two:
1. To learn more about your adaptive behavior, healthy and unhealthy.
2. To identify, accept, embrace, and nurture your adaptive behavior parts, which are ways of being that have helped you survive.
3. To better understand how your unhealthy adaptive behaviors have contributed to the difficulties in your relationships.
4. To get to know yourself and others in the class better by sharing openly in small groups.
5. To begin to understand the value of building a support network both inside and outside the class
6. To learn and use affirmations that will help your process.

Agenda for Session Two:
6:45 to 7:00 p.m. Arrive, greet new friends, get a hug, and a cup of tea or coffee.

7:00 to 7:10 p.m. Relaxation Exercise - "Breathing through our fears."

7:10 to 7:45 p.m. Small groups led by volunteer helpers. Suggested questions:
- How did your week go?
- Were you able to do the homework of calling three other people? How did it feel to make
- calls? How did it feel to receive calls?
- What was your reaction to taking the *Fisher Divorce Adjustment Scale*?
- What did you learn from the "Adaptation" chapter?

7:45 to 8:30 p.m. Presentation on "Adaptive Behavior."

8:30 to 8:45 p.m. Break.

8:45 to 9:00 p.m. Talk about homework assignments and meeting place for next week. Turn in *Fisher Divorce Adjustment Scale* answer sheets, Personal Information Sheets, and Registration Agreements (if not done last week).

9:00 to 9:50 p.m. Small group discussion of the "Adaptive Behavior" presentation, and the "Adaptation" chapter in *Rebuilding: When Your Relationship Ends*. Sample questions:
- What kinds of adaptive behaviors did you learn as a child?
- What kind of adaptive behaviors did you use in your last love relationship? What kind of adaptive behaviors did your former love partner do?
- How did your unhealthy adaptive behavior cause you difficulty in your last relationship?
- What feelings have kept you stuck in rigid adaptive behavior?
- What can you do to nurture and take care of yourself this week?

9:50 to 10:00 p.m. Big group time and closure. Time for "I feel ____" messages.

Homework For Next Week's Seminar: (* Indicates most important homework)
*1. Read Chapter 8 "Grief" in *Rebuilding*.
*2. Call at least three people on the class list to get to know each other and create your support network.
*3. Do the homework suggested on the Adaptive Behavior Homework Sheet (p. 10).
 4. Read Chapter 5 on "Loneliness," Chapter 6 on "Friendship," and Chapter 7 on "Guilt/Rejection" if you have time.

Adaptive Behavior Homework Sheet

Make a list of healthy, natural, and authentic behaviors.
Here are some examples mentioned in the Rebuilding Seminar "Adaptation" session. Examples: (1) Expressing feelings (2) Nurturing yourself (3) Asking for what you want and need (4) Being vulnerable with people around you (5) Asking questions (6) Having fun. Continue your own list and start thinking about what are healthy and healing behaviors.

Identify which of the above healthy traits (from your own list) were affirmed, encouraged, and supported at home or by your family of origin.
This is a difficult question helping you to look more closely at your childhood. When you didn't get your needs met in natural, authentic ways, you likely developed adaptive ("survivor") behaviors. The behaviors you chose were probably the best ones for your situation.

Identify some common adaptive behaviors and suggested homework for each:
1. If you identified yourself as **perfectionist** in your past relationship(s), your homework is to do less compulsive behavior. Examples: leave your bed unmade; let the dishes stack up a little.
2. If you identified yourself as an **over-responsible** person in your past relationship(s), your homework is to ask someone to do something for you and to say "no" when someone asks you to do something for them.
3. If you identified yourself as a **logical, rational** adult person in your past relationship(s), your homework is to say "I feel" messages every day and list as many feelings as you can each time.
4. If you identified yourself as a **people pleaser** in your past relationship(s), your homework is to figure out some homework to do on your own which will please *you* and help you build an identity of your own by tuning in to your own wants and needs.
5. If you identified yourself as having **other adaptive behaviors,** determine appropriate homework designed to help you experiment with becoming more authentic or balanced.
6. **If you don't know which adaptive-survivor behavior you have been doing**, your homework is to do all five of these homework assignments to see which are the most difficult for you. Those are the ones you need to work on the most.

Identify the underlying feelings or unmet needs from your childhood.
When you do this homework, pay attention to which one of the following six feelings seem to motivate your adaptive behavior. These six are guilt, rejection, fear, low self-worth, anger, or learned behavior (the urge to automatically behave in ways you learned as a child). Realize that you will have difficulty being authentic until you work through these six feelings. You can minimize these feelings by learning to give to yourself the love, nurturing and support you may not have received as a child. These are some suggestions of things to do to minimize these feelings:
1. **Guilt:** Put up a sign that says, "I'm Not Responsible" and read it daily.
2. **Rejection:** Have a friend or loved one write a list of ten or more things they like about you. Read the list until you believe it.
3. **Fear:** Write out a list of your fears. Share this list with a trusted person.
4. **Low self-worth:** Make a list of ten things you like about yourself. Read the list until you start to believe that the things you wrote are true.
5. **Anger:** Write "I am angry at you because..." as many times as possible. Then rewrite the list with "I am angry at myself because...."
6. **Learned behavior:** Make a list of the "shoulds" you learned as a child. Read each one and if you don't agree with it, rewrite it into something you do believe. Example: "Always eat everything on your plate" might be changed to, "I don't have to eat everything on my plate when I am on a diet," or "It's OK to stop eating when I'm full."

get when you were young. Nurture and take care of yourself in
hing nice for yourself such as eating an ice cream cone, taking a
k, reading a good book, getting a sun tan, and giving yourself a
some new ways of behaving. Be as authentic and honest as you
self; criticizing yourself usually won't help! Change takes time
f lots of encouragement! Read and practice saying to yourself the
itled "101 Ways to Praise a Child."

es on during the presentation in Session Two on Adaptation.

List of Adaptive Behaviors

Here is a partial list of adaptive behaviors — there are many more. You may have chosen one or more of these behaviors to help you survive, adapt, or to make the most of your childhood situation. Of all the possible behaviors you could have chosen, you probably chose the best one for you, considering the environment you grew up in. The behavior usually worked well in your childhood but it doesn't work as well in your adult relationships.

Adults tend to become more balanced, often by attracting people with different behaviors. If you chose one of the behaviors from the list below, you probably chose a person to be in relationship with that has a behavior from the opposite list. You thought you chose a love partner because you fell in love. Maybe you fell in love with a behavior in another that you have not yet developed in yourself. After the honeymoon period in your love relationship, you may dislike a behavior in another that you have not learned to develop or accept in yourself.

These adaptive behaviors aren't necessarily bad. It's only when they are rigid or extreme that they become a problem. Many of these behaviors protected you. If you felt pain, anger, fear, or hurt as a child, you needed to find ways to protect yourself. The process of taking charge of your life begins with your awareness of your behavior. Because this behavior often started when you were feeling pain, you may feel pain when you start recognizing and owning these parts of yourself. Healing usually occurs when you embrace your pain and decide to learn from it.

Because you developed these behaviors to compensate for unmet needs, you can continue your healing by learning to meet these unmet needs. Over-responsible people have learned to be good givers but usually have trouble taking. Start giving to yourself in the same manner you have been giving to others. When you start attempting to become responsible for yourself instead of being over-responsible for everyone else you usually will perceive yourself as being selfish. We suggest you look at this as *self-care* rather than selfish. Learning to nurture yourself will diminish your need for adaptive behavior.

To summarize, awareness will help you identify your adaptive behaviors, which will lead toward more authentic behavior. So, pay attention! Notice how you behave in your relationships with others. Be honest with yourself. Embracing any pain you may feel will help the pain become your teacher and help you discover your need for nurturing. You'll develop more self-respect and you may find it takes less effort to be authentic. The end result is that you will enjoy your life instead of adapting in order to survive.

Aggressive	vs.	Passive	Let's be logical	vs.	Off the wall
Over responsible	vs.	Under responsible	Fighter	vs.	Runner
Perfectionist	vs.	People pleaser	Blamer	vs.	I'm to blame
Controller	vs.	Rebellious	Clown	vs.	Invisible
Good Shepherd	vs.	Black sheep	Judge	vs.	Chameleon
Urge to help	vs.	I need help	Do it myself	vs.	Help me
Loves too much	vs.	Play it cool	Over-doer	vs.	Procrastinator
Smother mother	vs.	Wounded child	Work-aholic	vs.	Laid back
Superman	vs.	Lois Lane	Treadmill	vs.	Let's have fun
Superwoman	vs.	Casper Milquetoast	Complainer	vs.	Checks out
Intimidate	vs.	Martyr	It's your fault	vs.	It's my fault
Competitor	vs.	I can't	Gambler	vs.	Don't rock the boat
Caretaker	vs.	Victim	Whiner	vs.	Suffer in silence
Know it all	vs.	I don't know	Organizer	vs.	Disorganized
Criticizes others	vs.	Takes in criticism	Life of the party	vs.	Shy
Flame thrower	vs.	Asbestos suit	Center of attention	vs.	Withdrawn
Optimist	vs.	Pessimist	Confronter	vs.	Avoider
Righteous	vs.	I'm not okay	Enabler	vs.	Drug abuser

Authentic and Adaptive / Survivor Behaviors

This chart shows a continuum of five adaptive/survivor contrasted with more authentic behaviors. The goal is to grow from adaptive/survivor behavior towards authentic behavior.

Adaptive / Survivor Behavior	Authentic Behavior
Perfectionist Expects perfection in others Provides rigid limits to others Wants to look good Strives for perfection Hooks defensive response in others Makes others feel not OK Wants to change another Never enough	**Strives for Excellence** Gives constructive feedback to others Provides healthy limits to others Not concerned with appearances Strives for excellence Hooks appropriate response in others Helps others to feel OK Accepts others Satisfied with accomplishments
Over-responsible Smother-mother Gives another a fish Giving is self serving Hooks adaptive response in others Makes others feel not OK Controlling Caretaker Enabler Feels selfish when taking care of self	**Responsible to Self** Empathetic nurturing Teaches another to fish Giving is unselfish Hooks natural response in others Helps others to feel OK A catalyst to another's growth Caregiver Tough love Is able to do self-care
Rational-Logical Rigid Unable to access feelings Uses only facts and interpretations Dictator Makes others feel not OK Uses learned survival strategies Concerned with doing it the right way Expresses opinions, tries to convince others	**Thoughts and Feelings Balanced** Flexible Able to access feelings Uses all sub-personality parts Chairman of the board Makes others feel OK Makes loving choices Concerned about others Expresses beliefs and listens to others
Rebel Wants own way, rebellious Upsets system Behavior results in more chaos Concerned with rebelling Selfish manipulation Hooks criticism in others	**Healthy Identity** Able to bring about change Helps system work better Behavior results in efficiency and effectiveness Adjusts to situation Positive manipulation Hooks support in others
Needy and Hurt Child Mimics others Pretends to have a good time Expresses what others feel and express Concerned about fitting in Follower Hooks rescuing in others	**Natural and Creative child** Creative and spontaneous Fun loving Expresses feelings easily Inner directed Leader Hooks spontaneity in others

It is Never My Responsibility to:

Give what I really don't want to give
Sacrifice my integrity to anyone
Do more than I have time to do
Drain my strength for others
Listen to unwise counsel
Retain an unfair relationship
Be anyone but exactly who I am
Conform to unreasonable demands
Be one-hundred percent perfect
Follow the crowd
Submit to overbearing conditions
Meekly let life pass me by
It is never my responsibility to give up who I am to anyone
for fear of abandonment.

— Author Unknown

When I Feel Responsible ...

FOR Others	TO Others
I fix	I show empathy
I protect	I encourage
I rescue	I share
I control	I confront
I carry their feelings	I level with them
I don't listen	I listen
I am insensitive	I am sensitive
***	***
I feel tired	I feel relaxed
I feel anxious	I feel free
I feel fearful	I feel aware
I feel liable	I feel high self-esteem
***	***
I am concerned with:	*I am concerned with*:
the solution	relating person to person
answers	feelings
circumstance	the person
being right	discovering truth
details	the big picture
performance	relating
***	***
I am a manipulator.	I am a helper guide.
I expect the person to	I expect the person to be
live up to my expectations.	responsible for self.
I feel fearful and hang on.	I can trust and let go.

Words of Wisdom to "Rescuers"

A *rescuer* is a person who creates relationships with someone who *needs* rescuing. It feels so good for the rescuer to find someone to rescue, and it feels so good for the person needing rescuing, that often the two people end up being in a committed relationship with each other; an *over-responsible person* in relationship with an *under-responsible* person. I taught about 2,000 people ending a relationship in the Rebuilding class and the majority of them described their last relationship as an over- and under-responsible relationship.

You rescuers can easily believe you are "superior" to those who need rescuing. You believe you are doing all of these wonderful things that will get you brownie points in Heaven. It's true the things you get done are impressive. You are doing many kind deeds to, and for, others. Many times you provided an environment that allowed the other person to make tremendous personal growth. However, it is helpful to realize that your *rescuing* is often *controlling* others, keeping them smaller, weaker, dependent, and unable to do things for themselves. Your need to rescue someone means you will have to keep them in need of rescuing.

How did you become a rescuer? During your formative years, your emotional development became stunted. You stopped getting all of your needs met. You compensated by finding another little child in someone else who had also stopped growing. You began to give to them the things you were wishing someone would give to you. It made you feel better but it set up a dangerous precedent. You began being so involved in helping another that you were able to avoid looking at how much you needed to take care of yourself. You began the development of an adaptive-survivor part in order to feel better and get more of your needs met.

There are a wide variety of situations that could have encouraged you to develop a rescuer pattern of behavior. Sometimes you felt frustrated because you weren't getting enough attention or love. Sometimes you learned you could manipulate your environment by developing adaptive behaviors. Sometimes you felt very criticized and became adaptive to feel better instead of feeling not okay. Sometimes you suffered from a lack of parenting because your parents were not around or were especially weak in parenting skills. Sometimes everyone around you were under-responsible, perhaps even in an altered state due to drugs of some sort. You learned to be an over-responsible rescuer in order to keep your family functioning.

If you were to make a list of the many adaptive/survivor behaviors you could have chosen, being a rescuer was probably the best choice you could have made. It helped you make the most of your situation. It not only helped you to get more needs met, it often was very helpful to the people around you. It worked well in your formative years. It doesn't work as well in your adult relationships.

Relationships that are over/under often become stressful and sometimes end. Rescuers often become emotionally drained. The last stage of the relationship usually includes anger because you have given so much and received so little. You aren't able to see your contribution to the problem. You have difficulty taking so even if they tried to give to you, you would have trouble receiving. For you, it is easier to give than receive.

The system of interaction between the two people can become upset. Here are some examples. The couple have a baby and the rescuer is too busy with the baby to continue rescuing the partner. The rescuer finds a stronger identity by doing self-care. (This always feels selfish to rescuers when they start becoming responsible to self instead of over-responsible.) The person who is under-responsible becomes tired of being controlled and either leaves the relationship or becomes more responsible for self in the relationship. Any one of these "upsetting-the-system behaviors" can contribute to the ending of the relationship. If asked, you can usually identify when the system began to change. This can be the beginning of the end of your relationship. It is possible to change within the relationship without it ending, but both parties have to have awareness plus good communication to do this.

Leaving the relationship will not help rescuers to change. Instead you will probably find another person needing rescuing and create another over/under relationship. The challenge is to change the relationship with yourself by learning to become responsible for self instead of being either over- or under-responsible. It usually includes learning to take emotionally, instead of always emotionally giving to another. It means giving to yourself the things that you didn't get enough of in your formative years.

Think of the wonderful things that could happen if you transformed your well-developed "giving to others part" into a "giving to yourself part." You might find the happiness, contentment, and inner peace that you deserve. Good luck on your journey.

— Bruce

101 Ways To Praise A Child

These comments are good to share with your children, but they are also healing for you to say to yourself.

A big hug.
A-1 job.
A big kiss.
Awesome.
Beautiful.
Beautiful work.
Beautiful sharing.
Bingo.
Bravo.
Creative job.
Dynamite.
Excellent.
Exceptional performance.
Fantastic.
Fantastic job.
Good for you.
Great discovery.
Good.
Good job.
Great.
Hot dog.
How smart.
Hooray for you.
How nice.
Hip, hip, hooray.
I like you.
I trust you.
I respect you.
I knew you could do it.
I'm proud of you.
Looking good
Magnificent.
Marvelous.

My buddy.
Now you're flying.
Neat.
Nice work.
Now you've got it.
Nothing can stop you now.
Outstanding
Outstanding performance.
Phenomenal.
Remarkable.
Say, I love you.
Spectacular.
Super.
Super star.
Super job.
Super work.
Terrific.
That's correct.
That's incredible.
That's the best.
Way to go.
Wow.
What an imagination.
What a good listener.
Well done.
You are fun.
You are exciting.
You are responsible.
You believe.
You figured it out.
You mean a lot to me.
You make me happy.
You tried hard.

You made my day.
You make me laugh.
You mean the world to me.
You brighten my day.
You learned it right.
You care.
You're a winner.
You're growing up.
You're special.
You're important.
You're on target.
You're on your way.
You've got a friend.
You're wonderful.
You're spectacular.
You're perfect.
You're darling.
You're precious.
You're a joy.
You're a treasure.
You're catching on.
You're beautiful.
You're unique.
You've discovered the secret.
You're on top of it.
You're incredible.
You're a real Trouper.
You're important.
You're sensational.
You're a good friend.
You're A-OK.
You're fantastic.

PS: Remember, a smile is worth a thousand words.

Risks

To laugh is to risk appearing the fool.

To weep is to risk appearing sentimental.

To reach out to another is to risk involvement.

To expose feelings is to risk exposing your true self.

To place your ideas, your dreams before a crowd is to risk their loss.

To love is to risk not being loved in return.

To live is to risk dying.

To hope is to risk despair.

To try is to risk failure.

But risks must be taken, because the greatest hazard in life is to risk nothing.

The person who risks nothing, does nothing, has nothing and is nothing.

They may avoid suffering and sorrow but they cannot learn, feel, change, grow, love, live.

Chained by their certitude's they are a slave, they have forfeited their freedom.

Only a person who risks is free.

– Author Unknown

A hug is a great gift.
One size fits all,
and it's easy to exchange.

Affirmations

Writing and saying affirmations out loud can be a powerful experience. Here are some examples of affirmations. We invite you to write one or more affirmations that are important for you in your own personal growth and self-actualization. Post them in a prominent place and say them out loud at least once a day.

1. I am making this crisis into a creative experience.
2. I am learning new and healthier ways of interacting with others.
3. I am taking charge of my life and creating the happiness I deserve.

My first affirmation is:

My second affirmation is:

My third affirmation is:

My reactions to the reading assignment in *Rebuilding* are:

My reactions to the Adaptation session of the Rebuilding Seminar:

What were some of the important things I learned in Session Two?

What are some of the important changes I am making in my thinking and my actions?

Journal (See note on page 6.)

Session Three
Grief

"There's This Terrible Feeling of Loss"

Grief is an important part of your divorce process. You need to work through grief's emotions in order to let go of the dead love relationship. An intellectual grasp of the stages of grief can help you become emotionally aware of grief. Then you can do the grieving that you may have been afraid of before.

Lesson Plan For Session Three
Grief: There's This Terrible Feeling of Loss

Goals for Session Three:
1. To understand the process of grieving your loss(es).
2. To become aware of and understand the symptoms of your grief.
3. To give yourself permission to grieve as much and as long as you need to.
4. To learn the importance of self-care during your grief process.
5. To write a "good-bye letter," letting go of your past relationship(s).
6. To understand how to do "grief management."
7. To make an agreement with other group members to call someone if you're feeling really down or suicidal.
8. To understand the results of your *Fisher Divorce Adjustment Scale.*
9. To learn and use affirmations that will help you work through your grief process.

Agenda for Session Three:

6:45 to 7:00 p.m. Arrive, greet new friends, get a hug, and a cup of tea or coffee.

7:00 to 7:15 p.m. Centering and Connecting Exercise. Discuss lesson plans.

7:15 to 7:45 p.m. Small group discussion. What are the losses you're experiencing right now? What are you afraid you'll lose? How are these losses affecting you in terms of the feelings you're having? What kinds of losses are your children going through? What are some losses you've experienced in the past? How did your week go? What did you learn from the experience of doing the adaptive behavior homework? (see last week's lesson plans) Which of the six underlying feelings of guilt, rejection, fear, anger, low self-concept, or learned behavior are keeping you stuck in rigid, adaptive behavior?

7:45 to 8:00 p.m. Share the results of the *Fisher Divorce Adjustment Scale* scoring.

8:00 to 8:15 p.m. Discuss suicidal feelings and do a "no-suicide pact" with the group.

8:15 to 8:30 p.m. Break.

8:30 to 9:00 p.m. Lecture and presentation on grief and grief symptoms. Talk about writing the good-bye letter. Read a grief good-bye letter. Music.

9:00 to 9:55 p.m. Small group exercise. Spend about 20 minutes writing a good-bye letter. Write it to your former love-partner if possible. Otherwise, write it to the biggest loss you are ready to say good-bye to: pets, home, neighbors, husband or wife role, your old self, an old loss, etc. Read your letter to the other members of your small group, if you're willing, or have someone else read it out loud for you.

9:55 to 10:00 p.m. "Huggle-time" and closure. Time for "I feel _____" messages.

Homework For Next Week's Seminar: (* Indicates Most Important Homework)
*1. Read Chapter 9, "Anger" in *Rebuilding.*
*2. Let yourself grieve as much as you need to. If necessary manage your grief by setting aside some time to really let go and sob uncontrollably.
3. Call one or more group members for support in your grief process.
4. Write more good-bye letters to the biggest losses of love that you're ready to let go of. (We don't recommend that you send these letters, they're designed to help you grieve and heal.)
5. Continue nurturing yourself by doing some things that make you feel good this week.
6. Continue to do the homework on your adaptive behavior. (Example: asking someone to do something for you, or saying no when someone asks you to do something for them.)
7. Read Chapter 7, "Guilt & Rejection" in *Rebuilding* if you have enough time and energy.

Life Stress and Physical Illness

Thomas H. Holmes and Richard H. Rahe conducted research that shows a connection between life stress and physical illness. The stress is either from internal sources or external sources; it is irrelevant where it originates. The stress comes from major changes in our lives and if the change is important enough, it may cause a crisis. If we do not adjust, there is an increased chance that a major physical illness will occur within two years after the crisis!

After researching about 5,000 people, they arrived at the following formula. The total life change units is calculated from the chart below, by adding up the number of change events that occur within a six-month period of a person's life.

Total Life Change Units	Percentage of Major Illness Within Two Years
150 LCU's	20% to 30%
300 LCU's	40% to 50%
450 LCU's	60%
600 LCU's	80%

Conclusion: Increasing your ability to cope with stress, will decrease your chances of having a major illness.

Social Readjustment Rating Scale

Rank	Life Event	Mean Value LCU's	Rank	Life Event	Mean Value LCU's
1	Death of Spouse	100	22	Change of Responsibilities at Work	29
2	Divorce	73	23	Son/Daughter Leaving Home	29
3	Marital Separation	65	24	Trouble with In-Laws	29
4	Jail Term	63	25	Outstanding Personal Achievement	28
5	Death of Close Friend or Family Member	24 / 63	26	Wife Begins or Stops School	26
6	Personal Injury or Illness	53	27	Begin or End School	26
7	Marriage	50	28	Change in Living Conditions	25
8	Fired from Job	47	29	Revision of Personal Habits	24
9	Marital Reconciliation	45	30	Trouble with Boss	23
10	Retirement	45	31	Change in Work Hours/Conditions	5
11	Change in Health of Family	44	32	Change in Residence	20
12	Pregnancy	40	33	Change in Schools	20
13	Sex Difficulties	39	34	Change in Recreation	19
14	Gain of New Family Member	39	35	Change in Church Activities	19
15	Business Readjustment	39	36	Change in Social Activities	18
16	Change in Financial State	38	37	Mortgage or Loan less than $10,000	17
17	Death of a Close Friend	37	38	Change in Sleeping Habits	16
18	Change to Different Line of Work	36	39	Change in Number of Family Get-Togethers	15
19	Change in Number of Arguments w/Spouse	35	40	Change in Eating Habits	15
20	Mortgage Over $10,000	31	41	Vacation	13
21	Foreclosure/Loan or Mortgage	30	42	Christmas	12
			43	Minor Violations of the Law	11

Reference:
Holmes, Thomas H. and Rahe, Richard H. "The Social Readjustment Rating Scale," *Journal of Psychosomatic Research*, Vol. II, No. 2, August, 1967, pp. 213-218

Use this page to take notes on during the presentation in Session Three on Grief

Letting Go

Letting go does not mean to stop caring,
it means I can't do it for someone else.

Letting go is not to cut myself off,
it's the realization I can't control another.

Letting go is not to enable,
but to allow learning from natural consequences.

Letting go is to admit powerlessness,
which means the outcome is not in my hands.

Letting go is not to try to change or blame another,
it's to make the most of myself.

Letting go is not to care for,
but to care about.

Letting go is not to fix,
but to be supportive.

It's not to judge,
but to allow another to be a human being.

Letting go is not to be in the middle arranging the outcome,
but to allow others to affect their own destinies.

Letting go is not to be protective,
it's to permit another to face reality.

Letting go is not to deny,
but to accept.

Letting go is not to nag, scold or argue,
but instead to search out my own shortcomings and correct them.

Letting go is not to adjust everything to my own desires,
but to take each day as it comes and cherish myself in it.

Letting go is not to criticize and regulate anybody,
but to try to become what I dream I can be.

Letting go is not to regret the past
but to grow and live for the future.

Letting go is to fear less and live more.

— Author Unknown

Then, Now, Tomorrow

Then *was the past.* Now *is the present.* Tomorrow *will be the future.*

Then *was memories, both good and bad It was friends of old.
It was happiness and understanding. It was failures, success and compromise.*

You cannot live in the Then. *You must hold onto the good and learn
from the bad. You must remember the success and understand the failures.
You must use them to grow and become a more complete person.*

Now *is painful. It is remembering the past, no matter how hard you try
not to.* Now *is looking at failures with a piercing mind. Success is hard to
measure, or comprehend.* Now *is recovery, thinking about life.*

You have to always live in the Now. *Everyday is* Now, *the present.
Decisions made* Now *will affect your tomorrow.* Now *is the present,*
Now *is the past,* Now *is the future. All these things are rolled into one,* NOW.

Tomorrow *is what will become. Happiness, sorrow, pain and LOVE.
Will we be happy tomorrow? No one really knows that, but it can be determined.*

Tomorrow *is dreams, hopes and prayers. It is change, for better or worse
this change will come.*

Tomorrow. *It must come or life becomes stagnate like a lifeless pond on
the prairie of desolation.*

Tomorrow *is what you make of it.*

— Author Unknown

25

Dear Jane,

Even though it will probably only take you five minutes to read this, if you read it at all, it took me a long time to write it. It also took a lot of courage to speak my mind and my heart. I hope you don't see this as an attack on you, its not. Forgive me for my anger, its necessary. Anger is like a fire — I had to get it out and burn it up, so that I can be rid of it. I'm not trying to hurt you in any way. I know you've been hurt deeply already. I can't undo that, but I'm truly sorry. I've been hurt too, and I'm doing my best to forgive. I don't hold you responsible for my pain.

This is a letter to you, but not for you, it's for me. It's just a part of the work that I needed to do, so that I can get on with my life.   Good-bye.

Good-bye attorney's fees and custody battle

Good-bye frustration, wondering, waiting, never knowing

Good-bye foolish wishes and dreams

Good-bye to a marriage that was destined to fail, even before it began

Good-bye to the bitching when you couldn't get your way

Good-bye anger, at me, whether or not I had it coming

Good-bye sex, when you felt it

Good-bye trying to please you, which was practically impossible

Good-bye threats — who cares?!

Good luck kids, sorry you have to live with her for now

Good-bye insanity when my frustrations and anger overcame me

Good-bye your way, hello my way!

Good-bye being manipulated because I allowed myself to be

Good-bye feeling worthless, no matter what I did

Good-bye fear of what you'd do next

Good-bye looking for love elsewhere, and wishing I could come home to it

Good-bye "glimmer of hope" that someday it will work out

Good-bye pouring my heart out to you and feeling like you just didn't care

Good-bye craving to be loved by the woman I loved

Good-bye fear of failing, hello to being human

Good-bye abstinence

Good-bye resistance to every change I wanted

Good-bye to you planting a garden and me having to take care of it

Good-bye to being married once and having it work out

Good-bye to raising a family together

Good-bye to sticking together through thick and thin

Good-bye to no help from you, sometimes when I really needed it

Good-bye to your family, whom I grew to love

Good-bye to being an uncle to your sister's kid

Which reminds me, good-bye to your sister who will probably always take advantage of you

Good-bye to trying to understand your anger, maybe you were born with it

Good-bye to your hugs, which I'd die for when I could get them

Good-bye to growing old together

Good-bye to retiring to our mountain home together, my life long dream

Good-bye to my mother's friend, she really loved you, you know

Good-bye to our lake, and the happiest times of my life

Good-bye to catching fish with you there, 'til our arms hurt

Good-bye to hearing our kids saying "Mommy & Daddy" all in one sentence

Good-bye to being there as a team for them for the rest of our lives

Good-bye to being there, at home, for them whenever they need me

Hello to being a weekend father — great! Just what I've always dreamed of

Good-bye to the chance to put them to bed every night, reading books together, saying prayers and telling them I love them

Good-bye to showing them by example how two people can work it out, pray together and stay together and love their way through any problem no matter what

"Till death do us part" — the truth is, our marriage has died, and with it a part of me has died too. Now I'm alone, one of the "walking wounded"

Good-bye to loving you — damn, that's hard to say! But, there's no point in it now, what's the use?

Thank you Lord for the tears to wash away the pain, I've got to go on now. I can't believe how hard this is, but in a way it feels good to let go.

Someday, I've got to have faith that someday, I'll be healed. I wish you the best with all my heart.

Good-bye Letters

Dear Tony,

Good-bye to wonderful memories. Good-bye to a bitter ending.

Good-bye to our morning showers — together. What a wonderful way we started the day!

Good-bye to filling our photo album — family pictures — of yours and mine.

Good-bye to feeling secure in a blanket of love. Although our vows had not been "traditional,"
"our life" felt so very real.

Good-bye to the puppy's kisses, and our early-morning ritual of dog bones and tricks that we quietly shared,
while my love lingered in dreams and the warmth of our bed.

Good-bye to my fish friends. I will miss your enthusiasm and joy when you hungrily saw me. Will you miss me?

Good-bye to a house that felt like mine — but wasn't — nor ever would be.

Good-bye to the adventurous couple — partners — the team.

Good-bye to hearing "How's My Babe?" You could make me feel so special with your smile!

Oh my love, I never got to say good-bye — with you — and be reaffirmed that our
relationship had been meaningful. And it was, you know, so very meaningful to me.

Good-bye to my once best friend — and thoughts of "What did I do?" or "could have done."

Good-bye to the anger you have for me. Who are you really angry at?

> You know my only crime was loving you.

So Good-bye and Happy Holidays —

May your New Year be filled with love, happiness, tenderness, trust, courage, truth, and
especially, peace of heart and peace of mind.

Good-bye to pain. I've learned — first hand — it doesn't have to last so long,
but love can last forever — or for however long you believe you can love.

Our memories, our caring, and my hope for our future — I sealed them away in a tomb
in my heart. Someday, when I am ready, I will remember how special it was,
and you will be there for as long as I have that heart.

But now, most of all...

Good-bye to who I thought I was — your lover — your "other half" — your cook — your maid

> She doesn't exist anymore. A much stronger, wiser, independent, witty, beautiful,

> > and very stalwart, cautious woman took her place.

I like her — she's fun!

> And you know what? She doesn't need anyone to be that way,

> > but I don't think she ever really did — she just didn't know it.

> Good-bye to what once was — today is today — and welcome future, with love!

> Good-bye, my Babe. So long.

Affirmations

Writing and saying affirmations out loud can be a powerful experience. Here are some examples of affirmations. We invite you to write one or more affirmations that are important for you in your own personal growth and self-actualization. Post them in a prominent place and say them out loud at least once a day.

1. I am ready to acknowledge and grieve the losses I'm experiencing in my life.
2. I am committed to investing more in the relationship with myself so that I can become the person I am capable of becoming.
3. I am strong enough emotionally to allow myself to grieve appropriately.
4. I am open and ready to learn how to love myself more.
5. I am committed to reaching out to others and asking for what I need and want.
6. I am simply feeling my feelings and that's perfectly natural.

My first affirmation is:

My second affirmation is:

My third affirmation is:

My reactions to the reading assignment in *Rebuilding* are:

My reactions to the Grief session of the Rebuilding class are:

What were some of the important things I learned in Session Three?

What are some of the important changes I am making in my thinking and my actions?

Journal (See note on page 6.)

Session Four
Anger
"Damn the S.O.B.!"

You'll feel a powerful rage when your love relationship ends, whether you're the dumpee or the dumper. Those angry feelings are a natural, healthy part of being human. How you express them makes all the difference. Don't bottle your feelings up inside, but you needn't get aggressive either. You can learn to express both your divorce anger and your "everyday" anger constructively. And you can learn to reduce your anger altogether.

Lesson Plan for Session Four
Anger — Damn the S.O.B.!

Goals for Session Four:
1. To begin to view anger not as an enemy of love, but as an ally of love.
2. To learn that anger can help to cleanse relationships by helping to resolve issues.
3. To learn how to reduce inappropriate anger in your life.
4. To discover some new skills for coping with anger.
5. To discover positive, appropriate ways to express anger.
6. To identify some of the other feelings associated with your anger.
7. To learn and use affirmations that will help you become more comfortable with your anger.

Agenda for Session Four:

6:45 to 7:00 p.m. Arrive, greet new friends, get a hug, and a cup of tea or coffee.

7:00 to 7:10 p.m. Connecting and centering exercise.

7:10 to 7:55 p.m. Presentation: Anger.

7:55 to 8:30 p.m. Large group "Body Sculpture" exercise. Facilitator(s) demonstrate all body sculptures. Participants then break into dyads and try body sculptures. Discuss with dyad partner your experience while doing the body sculptures. Talk openly with your partner during this exercise — really play the part as much as possible. Act out any other creative body sculptures you can identify from your previous relationship. Which body sculptures describe the way(s) you related to your former love-partner?

8:30 to 8:45 p.m. Break.

8:45 to 9:00 p.m. Talk about homework assignments for next week.

9:00 to 9:55 p.m. Small group exercise: Be sure to allow each person a chance to share.
- How do I express my anger? (Explode, somatize, feel angry at myself, depression, sarcasm, passive aggressive, denial, own it and talk it out, misdirect it toward the wrong person, etc.)
- If I'm not happy about the way I'm expressing anger, what would work better for me?
- If I'm stuffing anger, what ways will I begin to let it go?
- What behaviors or situations "push my buttons"?
- How did people in my family deal with anger when I was a child?
- What have I done to nurture and take care of myself this week?
- What other feelings are related to my anger? (Fear, frustration, rejection, guilt, loneliness, low self worth, etc.)
- What are my emotional blocks to expressing anger appropriately? (Nice guy, fear of rejection, anger is unhealthy, anger is destructive, etc.)
- What positive ways can I express and dissipate my anger that will not be harmful to me or to another?
- Share anger letters or other homework I've done that was important for me.

9:50 to 10:00 p.m. Big group time and closure. Time for "I feel _____" messages.

Homework For Next Week's Seminar: (*Indicates Most Important Homework)
*1. Reading assignment: Chapter 11, "Self-Worth" in *Rebuilding*.
*2. Write a list of ten things you like about yourself.
3. Call one or two people in the group and talk about adaptation, grief, and anger in your life.
4. Continue to nurture yourself by doing things you like to do.
5. Write "I am angry at you because _____!" as many times as you can. Do not share this writing with the person you are angry at. Instead, when you feel your anger is dissipated, go back over the letter and rewrite these anger statements into "I am angry at myself because _____!" Use anger as an avenue into understanding yourself better.
6. Use some of the new skills you've learned for expressing and coping with anger.
7. Read Chapter 10, "Letting Go" in the textbook.

Healthy Ways to Work On Anger

(This list was compiled by junior high children in a summer activities program.)

1. Take a time-out to cool down, then talk out the problem.

2. Run as fast as you can.

3. Sing.

4. Bounce a ball as hard as you can.

5. Punch a pillow/mat/grass.

6. Cry.

7. Yell into a pillow (or away from others).

8. Scribble.

9. Draw what you are angry about.

10. Write in a "feelings journal."

11. Shred newspapers.

12. Count to ten (or 20 or 100 or ...).

13. Stomp and storm (alone).

14. Pretend you are a balloon and take in a deep, slow breath, hold it to the count of three, and let it out slowly.

15. Talk to a friend.

16. Squish marshmallows.

17. Do any kind of exercise.

18. Listen to music.

19. Make noise with a whistle, wooden spoon and a pot, etc.

20. Make faces about how you feel.

Using Anger to Become More Empowered

Many of you who are ending a love relationship are afraid of angry feelings in yourself and others. You believe anger is aggressive, destructive, and harmful to self and others. The extreme rage you might be feeling I have called "angerism."

I had to learn that it is okay to be angry toward someone I love or have an important relationship with. I had to learn that anger can be empowering instead of aggressive, productive instead of destructive, healthy instead of harmful. Many people in your position ask how you can use your anger to become empowered.

Imagine the woman who has no college education, put her partner through graduate school, and kept hearing how inadequate she was because she was not "educated." When she becomes divorced, she might discover she is feeling a great deal of anger about her lack of education. She may use these angry feelings to become empowered and give herself the determination to find the time and money to obtain her own college degree.

Imagine the man who was informed many times he had no feelings. When the divorce comes, he discovers large fires of anger burning inside of him. He takes the Rebuilding class determined to learn to access and share his feelings of anger. He finds it empowering to talk about feelings and is grateful for the opportunity to transform his anger into emotional strength.

How about it? Can you find ways to use your anger to become a more powerful and self-actualized person? It is worth looking into. You might discover how good it feels to be able to control your life instead of carrying around a burden of anger that keeps you emotionally tired and overwhelmed.

— Bruce

Use this page to take notes on during the presentation in Session Four on Anger

Illustrating Relationships With Body Sculpturing

A body sculpture is a way of experiencing different kinds of relationships by placing your body in a way that models or sculptures a particular kind of relationship. Doing this exercise may help you to discover aspects of your past and present relationships. This exercise—based largely on the work of famed family therapist Virginia Satir—is experiential and more meaningful when you actually model these relationships with another person. I recommend doing it on anger night because it often helps participants to discover angry feelings.

The A-Frame Dependency Relationship

This is the dependency relationship where two people lean on each other because they have not learned to be whole single people by themselves. The dependency upon the other person some-times feels good, but it is somewhat confining. When one person wants to change and grow, it upsets the other person. Try to put into words some of the feelings that you have while you are assuming this position.

The Smothering Relationship

The smothering relationship is quite frequently seen in high school and teenage relationships. The vocabulary for this relationship is, "I cannot live without you. I want to spend the rest of my life with you. I will devote myself completely to making you happy. It feels so good to be so close to you." Many love relationships start with this kind of a smothering relationship. They may grow and change into another body sculpture position because there is not enough space for the two people to grow in this position. The emotional closeness of the smothering relationship may feel good for a while, but eventually you feel smothered and trapped.

The Pedestal Relationship

The pedestal relationship is about worshipping the other person and saying "I love you not for what you are but for what I think you are. I have an idealized image of you. I would like to have you live up to that image." It is very precarious being up on the pedestal because there are so many expectations from the other person. As with all of these relationships there are problems of communication. Because you are in love with the person's idealized image, you are looking up to and trying to communicate with that image instead of with the real person. There can be a great deal of emotional distancing in this relationship.

The Master-Slave Relationship

"I am the head of this family. I am the boss. I will make the decisions around here." This relationship is not necessarily the male being the boss and head of the family. There are many females who are masters in the family and make all of the decisions. Many relationships have one of the partners with a stronger and more powerful personality than the other. This is okay until the relationship becomes rigid and has no flexibility. If one person makes all of the decisions, then emotional distancing and inequality will most likely result. The rigid relationship tends to take a great deal of emotional energy maintaining one person as master and the other as slave. There is often a power struggle going on that interferes with the communication and intimacy of the relationship.

The Boarding House Relationship

These two people are linked together by their elbows with a marriage contract or a relationship agreement. There is little communication in this relationship. Often the people watch TV while they are eating and spend time apart for the remainder of the evening. Communication is especially difficult in this relationship. It is a loveless relationship in the sense that there is no expression of love towards each other. Again, when you try this position, notice that when one person moves forward, changes or grows and matures, the other person is linked to that growth. This makes it a confining relationship.

The Martyr Relationship

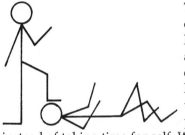

The martyr is the one on the hands and knees in the figure above and who completely sacrifices him or herself in trying to serve the other people in that family instead of taking time for self. We need to see and understand that the martyr position is a very controlling position. When the person on hands and knees moves, the other person who has a foot on the martyr is thrown off balance.

What emotion does the martyr use for gaining control? He/she controls through guilt. How can you be angry at the person who is doing everything for you, who is taking care of you completely? The martyr is very efficient at controlling people around him/her. It is very difficult to live with a martyr because you feel so guilty that you are unable to express your angry feelings and ask for what you want or need. Many of you have had a martyr parent.

Understanding the martyr relationship may help you learn to deal with your martyr parent.

The Healthy Love-Relationship

These are two people who are whole and complete and have found internal happiness within themselves. They are two upright people who are not leaning upon or tangled up with the other person. They have an abundance of life to share with the other person. These two people choose to *stay* together rather than having to *be* together. They can be emotionally close like the smothering position. They can walk hand in hand as they might do in co-parenting their children. They can move apart and have their own careers, lives and friends. They choose to stay together because of their love for each other rather than having or needing to stay together because of some unmet emotional needs. The healthy love-relationship is a relationship that gives both people the space to grow and become themselves.

Summary

Try these different positions with a friend and see how they feel. You may want to create another body sculpture to describe your relationship. Try to put into either spoken or written words, the feelings that you were experiencing while you were in each body position. Which of these positions describe your past or present love relationship? Did the healthy relationship feel uncomfortable? Many people state that their past love relationship went through almost all of the unhealthy body positions.

The reason for having you do this experiential exercise is to help you understand some of the difficulties that went on in your love relationship which may have been related to the angerism that you are presently feeling. Any of the above unhealthy body sculpture positions might result in feelings of anger.

So What Can I Do About My Anger?
(From Alberti and Emmons, *Your Perfect Right*. Reprinted with permission from the publisher.)

We'd like to offer you a simple, three-step method for dealing with anger in your life. We'd like to, but we can't. Anger is complex, and handling it is complex as well. Fortunately, however, there are some really helpful procedures which are of proven value. As it happens, they fall naturally within three general guidelines: (1) minimize anger in your life; (2) cope before you get angry; and (3) respond assertively when you get angry.

Minimize Anger in Your Life

Our first ten steps are borrowed from the Williams' recommendations in *Anger Kills*:

(1) Improve your relationships with others through community service, tolerance, forgiveness, even caring for a pet.

(2) Adopt positive attitudes toward life through humor, religion, acting as if today is your last day.

(3) Avoid overstimulation from chemicals, work stress, noise, traffic.

(4) Listen to others. Practice trusting others.

(5) Have a confidant. Make a friend, and talk regularly, even before you feel stress building.

(6) Laugh at yourself. You really are pretty funny, you know. (It goes with being human.)

(7) Meditate. Calm yourself. Get in touch with your inner being.

(8) Increase your empathy. Consider the possibility that the other person may be having a *really* bad day.

(9) Be tolerant. Can you accept the infinite variety of human beings?

(10) Forgive. Let go of your need to blame somebody for everything that goes wrong in life.

To the Williams' ten, we add two of our own to this "anger-in-your-life" section:

(11) Work toward resolution of problems with others in your life, not "victory."

(12) Keep your life clear! Deal with issues when they arise, when you feel the feelings — not after hours/days/weeks of "stewing" about it. When you can't deal with it immediately, arrange a specific time when you can and will!

Cope Before You Get Angry

Anger is a natural, healthy, non-evil human emotion and, despite our best efforts to minimize its influence in our lives, all of us will experience it from time to time, whether we express it or not. So, in addition to the steps above, you'll want to be prepared before anger comes:

(13) Remember that you are responsible for your own feelings. You can choose your emotional responses by the way you look at situations. As psychologists Gary McKay and Don Dinkmeyer put it, *How You Feel Is Up To You*.

(14) Remember that anger and aggression are not the same thing! Anger is a feeling. Aggression is a style of behavior. Anger can be expressed assertively — aggression is not the only alternative.

(15) Get to know yourself. Recognize the attitudes, environments, events, and behaviors which trigger your anger. As one wise person suggested, "Find your own buttons, so you'll know when they're pushed!"

(16) Take some time to examine the role anger is playing in your life. Make notes in your log about what sets you up to get angry, and what you'd like to do about it.

(17) Reason with yourself. (Another good idea from the "Williams collection.") Recognize that your response will not change the other person. You can only change yourself.

(18) Deflect your cynical thoughts. Williams suggests thought stopping, distraction, meditation.

(19) Don't "set yourself up" to get angry! If your temperature rises when you must wait in a slow line (at the bank, in traffic), find alternate ways to accomplish those tasks (bank by mail, find another route to work, use the time for problem solving).

(20) Learn to relax. Develop the skill of relaxing yourself, and learn to apply it when your anger is triggered. You may wish to take this a step further by "desensitizing" yourself to certain anger-invoking situations.

(21) Develop several coping strategies for handling your anger when it comes, including relaxation,

physical exertion, "stress inoculation" statements, working out resolution within yourself, and other procedures, such as those suggested by the Williams (items 1-10 above) and those we've noted in the box at the end of this chapter.

(22) Save your anger for when it's important. Focus instead on maintaining good relationships with others.

(23) Develop and practice assertive ways to express your anger, so these methods will be available to you when you need them. Be spontaneous when you can; don't allow resentment to build; state your anger directly; avoid sarcasm and innuendo; use honest, expressive language; let your posture, facial expression, gestures, voice tone convey your feelings; avoid name-calling, putdowns, physical attacks, one-upmanship, hostility; work toward resolution.

Now you've developed a healthy foundation for dealing with angry feelings. Go on to the following section and get ready to handle your anger when it comes.

Respond Assertively When You Get Angry

(24) Take a few moments to consider if this situation is really worth your time and energy, and the possible consequences of expressing yourself.

(25) Take a few more moments to decide if this situation is one you wish to work out with the other person, or one you will resolve within yourself.

(26) Apply the coping strategies you developed in step 21 above.

If you decide to take action:

(27) Make some verbal expression of concern (assertively).

(28) "Schedule" time for working things out. If you are able to do so spontaneously, fine; if not, arrange a time (with the other person or with yourself) to deal with the issue later.

(29) State your feelings directly. Use the assertive style you have learned in this book (see #23 above), with appropriate nonverbal cues (if you are genuinely angry, a smile is inappropriate!).

(30) Accept responsibility for your feelings. You got angry at what happened; the other person didn't "make" you angry.

(31) Stick to specifics and to the present situation. Avoid generalizing. Don't dig up the entire history of the relationship!

(32) Work toward resolution of the problem. Ultimately you'll only resolve your anger when you've done everything possible to resolve its cause.

Here are a few verbal expressions others have found useful for expressing anger:

"I'm very angry."
"I'm getting really mad."
"I strongly disagree with you."
"I get damn mad when you say that."
"I'm very disturbed by this whole thing."
"Stop bothering me."
"That's not fair."
"Don't do that."
"That really pisses me off."
"You have no right to do that."
"I really don't like that."
"I'm mad as hell, and I'm not going to take this anymore!"

Relationships Are My Teachers

It is easy to believe that others are responsible for your anger. "That person is a pain in the neck" is a common way of putting it. It is also easy to play the role of the victim and believe there is nothing you can do about the things that others are doing to you. This victim role often leads to stuffing anger and letting it smolder inside of you like the glowing embers of a campfire.

Instead of projecting the blame for your anger upon another, or believing there is nothing you can do about how they are making you angry, I suggest you think about each person being your relationship teacher. Each time you feel angry, think about the opportunity of using your anger to learn more about yourself. Take some responsibility for your anger. It's yours, not someone else's.

Where did you learn to be angry? What feelings are underneath your anger? What does it mean when another person pushes your buttons and you react emotionally to their behavior? Maybe the person that you feel angry around is actually helping you to access your feelings and learn about yourself. Maybe that person is your relationship teacher. Probably the relationship that is most stressful for you is your most important relationship teacher. Maybe one of your most important teachers is your ex!!

One of the great lessons you can learn when your relationship ends is learning about yourself through your feelings of anger. The person that you have been blaming because they are causing you so much anger, may be giving you a gift of pain. Can you embrace your anger and learn from it? Can that stressful relationship become your teacher helping you to become empowered? Can you change the "gift of pain" into a "gift?"

Have you thought about loneliness being one of your feelings underneath anger? Maybe feeling lonely is a passive and indirect way of feeling angry because it seems no one is there loving you, comforting you, and making you feel okay. I think I sometimes feel angry when I believe there is no one in the world who cares about me.

Maybe taking a journey back in time will be helpful to you in letting go of your anger. The reflection below, from an old friend of many years ago, is one of my favorite writings.

—Bruce

The Swing

Tonight I walked. It was warm, and something within me cried with tension and restlessness. So, I walked. My feet took me all around the town, past brightly lit houses with mothers doing dishes, and kids doing homework, and dads reading newspapers. And I walked. And I was alone, silent, unnoticed.

My feet took me to the old school playground — the one I hurry past every day on my way to classes. I chose my used-to-be favorite swing, and watched the last rose color left over at the earth's edge from the sunset.

I was alone — yet close to something I cannot define. I began to swing. I pushed myself off the ground and pulled with my legs, going higher and higher. I leaned way back, and moved dizzily through the air. My soul felt free. Free! And for a moment I was a child again. Happy, alive, beautiful. I plotted to slowly die down to a certain level, then bail out. The best part is bailing out.

Bailing out is when I'm able to fly — leaving my anger and loneliness behind. I wonder if my anger and loneliness are still swinging on that swing? I know when I bailed out, I felt more peaceful, happy, and contented.

—JoAnn

Affirmations

Writing and saying affirmations out loud can be a powerful experience. Here are some examples of affirmations. We invite you to write one or more affirmations that are important for you in your own personal growth and self-actualization. Post them in a prominent place and say them out loud at least once a day.

1. I can express my anger in healthy ways.
2. It's okay to be angry.
3. Anger can be empowering.
4. Anger comes from many different sources.

My first affirmation is:

My second affirmation is:

My third affirmation is:

My reactions to the reading assignment in *Rebuilding* are:

My reactions to the Anger session of the Rebuilding class are:

What were some of the important things I learned in Session Four?

What are some of the important changes I am making in my thinking and my actions?

Journal (See note on page 6.)

Session Five
Self-Worth

"Maybe I'm Not So Bad After All!!"

It is okay to feel good about yourself. You can learn to feel better about yourself, and thus gain strength to help you adjust better to a crisis. As you successfully adjust to a crisis, you will feel even better about yourself!

Lesson Plan for Session Five
Self-Worth: Maybe I'm Not So Bad After All

Goals for Session Five:

1. To understand how important your self-worth is and how it's related to every part of your life.
2. To improve your feelings of self-worth.
3. To learn to accept "warm fuzzies" from yourself and others.
4. To learn to give yourself "warm fuzzies" in order to improve your feelings of self-worth.
5. To learn and use affirmations that will help you improve your feelings of self-worth.

Agenda for Session Five:

6:45 to 7:00 p.m. Arrive, greet new friends, get a hug, and a cup of tea or coffee.

7:00 to 7:10 p.m. Centering and Connecting Exercise.

7:10 to 7:50 p.m. Small group exercise:
* Share list of ten or more things you like about yourself.
* Share a recent experience of feeling angry. How did you handle it? (If you're not happy with the way you handled it, how would you like to have handled it?)
* How did the above experience influence how you felt about yourself?
* Share something you did to nurture yourself this week.
* Share what you plan to do next week to nurture yourself.
* Share my "I am angry at you (me) because ___" list (homework from last week)
* How was your week?

7:50 to 8:20 p.m. Presentation: Self-Worth.

8:20 to 8:35 p.m. Break.

8:35 to 8:50 p.m. Talk about homework assignments for next week. Discuss feelings about journaling.

8:50 to 9:50 p.m. Warm fuzzy exercise.

9:50 to 10:00 p.m. Big group time and closure. Time for "I feel ___" messages.

Homework For Next Week's Seminar: (* Indicates Most Important Homework)
*1. Reading Assignment: Chapter 12 in *Rebuilding*, "Transition" (Read this one, there's a lot there!!)
*2. Read "Steps to Improving Your Feelings of Self-Worth" (page 42).
*3. Think of a behavior that you would like to change. Think of ways to change it by taking "baby steps" so that you make a specific change each day in your behavior. Keep it up for a week. Congratulate and reward yourself a lot. Share with a friend who'll encourage you. Next week think of another change you would like to make. Keep making positive changes for the rest of your life. It will help you to like yourself better and to improve your feelings of self-worth.
4. Write a list of ten or more things you like about another person, such as one of your relatives, son or daughter, or friend. Give the list to the person. (It could be a meaningful birthday or Christmas present.)
5. Practice the steps of improving your self-worth recommended in Chapter 11. Which of the steps are most important to you? Which one is the most difficult to do?
6. Read Chapter 15, "Trust" in *Rebuilding*.

Steps to Improving Your Feelings of Self-Worth

The Decision
"Whatever you think, so shall you be." The first step is deciding you really want to improve your feelings of self-worth. This is not a decision to be taken lightly because changing how you feel about yourself will change almost everything in your life.

Diminish Self-Judgments
I suggest you start your self-love process by making a list of all the negative messages you keep saying to yourself. Some examples might be "You are really stupid." "You are conceited." "You'll never amount to anything." (Note: self-judgments are usually "you" messages.) After you have made your list, try restating them into more positive messages. For example, you might change the one that says, "You're being selfish and self-centered" into "I'm learning do my self-care."

Make Your Relationships with Others More Loving
Most of us have relationships with others which may be destructive to feelings of self-worth. Sometimes these relationships are with spouses, family members, or close friends. You need to make these relationships more loving instead of letting them act in a negative way upon your self-concept. You need to do one of three things: (a) end these relationships — difficult to do sometimes; (b) improve these relationships so they help you feel better about yourself; and (c) get so strong inside that such relationships cannot be destructive to your self-worth.

Learn to Give Yourself Affirmations
Make a list of ten or more things you like about yourself. Secondly, ask a close friend, family member, or lover to make a list of ten or more things he or she likes about you. Put these lists in place where you will read them every day, such as on your bathroom mirror. Read them until you start to believe them!

Learn to Accept and Believe Compliments
Have you ever tried to compliment a person with a low self-concept? Compliments run off them like water off a duck's back. The next time you receive a compliment say, "thank you," "that feels good," or "I never knew that." Concentrate on letting the compliment penetrate you as deeply as you can so you feel different deep inside.

Nurture Yourself on a Daily Basis
Take time to enjoy the sunsets, to meditate, to have quiet time by yourself or with someone else, to read something stimulating, to enjoy the flowers. Do something so that when you go to bed you can say, "Today I did this for myself."

And so it is! You are a special human being. Unique and different from anyone else. It is okay to like and love yourself. You are a loving — and lovable — person.

---

*Grant me the serenity
to accept the people I cannot change,
the courage
to change the one I can,
and the wisdom to know
it's ME!*

– Author Unknown

Use this page to take notes during the presentation of Session Five on Self-Worth.

Rules for Being Human

You will receive a body.
You may like it or hate it,
but it will be yours for your entire lifetime.

You will learn lessons.
You are enrolled in a full-time informal school called life.
Each day in this school you will have the opportunity to learn lessons.
You may like the lessons or think them irrelevant and stupid.

There are no mistakes, only lessons.
Growth is a process of trial, error and experimentation.
The "failed" experiments are as much a part of the process
as the experiment that ultimately succeeds.

A lesson is repeated until learned.
A lesson will be presented to you in various forms until you have learned it.
When you have learned it,
you can go on to the next lesson.

Learning lessons does not end.
There is no part of life that does not contain lessons.
If you are alive, there are lessons to be learned.

"There" is no better than "here."
When your "there" has become a "here,"
you will simply obtain another "there"
that will, again, look better than "here."

Others are merely mirrors of you.
You cannot love or hate something about another person
unless it reflects to you something you love or hate about yourself.

What you make of life is up to you.
You have all the tools and resources you need.
What to do with them is up to you.
The choice is yours.

Your answers lie inside you.
The answers to life's questions lie inside you.
All you need to do is look, listen, and trust.

— Author Unknown

I'm Okay — You're Okay

You start out your life being smaller, younger, weaker, less intellectual, and more dependent than those people around you. It is easy to believe you are "not okay" or "less okay" than those around you. If you don't experience enough love, nurturing, trust, and attention, you tend to stay in the "not okay" belief.

As you begin to grow and develop, you begin to learn the other basic "okay" positions. These are: "I'm not okay and neither are you"; "I'm okay and you're not okay"; "I'm not okay and you're okay." It would be interesting to understand why some people stay stuck in one of these positions and are not able to attain the ideal of "I'm okay and you're okay."

Presently you are taking control of your life which includes determining which "okay" position you tend to believe about yourself, and working towards becoming more okay. Sometimes you will have to accept that you are a human being with some "not okay" parts to you. Sometimes you can find enough self-love to love those parts that you used to not like about yourself. Sometimes it is okay to be "not okay."

As you are ending a love relationship, it is normal to discover some "not okay" feelings you have about yourself. They may be old leftovers from the past that need to be accepted for what they are — beliefs that were learned at an earlier stage of your growth and development. You learned them once — now maybe you can relearn what you learned earlier.

Do you believe it is possible to have a "corrective emotional experience?" Can you accept the nurturing from others in this class that are able to accept parts of you better than you can accept yourself? Can you learn to give to yourself the things you believe you didn't receive earlier in you life? Can you learn to take compliments and warm fuzzies from others when you are not sure you believe them yourself? Can you talk about and become vulnerable about your "not okay" feelings?

One of the valuable lessons you are learning in this class is that you can feel "more okay" than you may have felt in the past. We call that "turning a crisis into a creative experience."

—Bruce

Hugging

Hugging is healthy: It helps your body's immune system, it keeps you healthier, it helps cure depression, it reduces stress, it induces sleep, it's invigorating, it's rejuvenating, it has no unpleasant side effects. Hugging is nothing less than a miracle drug.

Hugging is all natural: It is organic, naturally sweet, no pesticides, no preservatives, no artificial ingredients and 100% wholesome.

Hugging is practically perfect: There are no movable parts, no batteries to wear out, no periodic checkups, low energy consumption, high energy field, inflation-proof, non-fattening, no monthly payments, no insurance requirements, theft-proof, nontaxable, non-polluting, one-size-fits all and, of course, fully returnable.

Affirmations:

Writing and saying affirmations out loud can be a powerful experience. Here are some examples of affirmations. We invite you to write one or more affirmations that are important for you in your own personal growth and self-actualization. Post them in a prominent place and say them out loud at least once a day.

1. I am a special person.
2. I like the way I feel about myself.
3. I accept myself unconditionally.

My first affirmation is:

My second affirmation is:

My third affirmation is:

My reactions to the reading assignment in *Rebuilding* are:

My reactions to the Self-Worth session of the Rebuilding class are:

What were some of the important things I learned in Session Five?

What are some of the important changes I am making in my thinking and my actions?

Journal (See note on page 6.)

Session Six
Transition

"I'm Waking Up and Putting Away My Leftovers"

Early experiences are extremely influential in our lives. The attitudes and feelings you developed in your childhood, and in relationships with family, friends, and lovers, are bound to carry over into new relationships. Some of these attitudes and feelings are helpful, others are not. If you are experiencing a personal identity-rebellion crisis, you may be seriously straining your love relationship. Recognize your valuable leftovers so you can keep and nourish them; work at changing those which get in the way.

Lesson Plan for Session Six
Transition: I'm Waking Up and Putting Away My Leftovers

Goals for Session Six:

1. To understand how "rebellion" may have affected your relationships.
2. To understand that *external rebellion* is an outward attempt to find one's identity, usually by acting out at someone who's perceived to be "parental."
3. To understand that *internal rebellion* is a process of working through inner-conflicts in order to create an identity separate from the expectations of others.
4. To help the partner of the person in rebellion to (a) grow and expand awareness instead of playing the victim role, and (b) to set appropriate boundaries with a rebellious person instead of acting "parental."
5. To give yourself permission to rebel when necessary in order to make positive changes.
6. To learn to use affirmations that will help you discover and maintain your own identity.
7. To explore how your childhood and family of origin influences may have contributed to the ending of your relationship.
8. To learn how "leftovers" and "power struggles" affect relationships.

Agenda for Session Six:

7:00 to 7:10 p.m. - Centering and Connecting Exercise.

7:10 to 7:45 p.m. - Small group sharing. What did you do this last week to improve your self-worth? What's a change in behavior that you could make this week that would really help you feel better about yourself? How are you doing at accepting compliments from others — not just being polite, but really taking them in? What changes in improving self-worth suggested in Chapter 11 did you make last week? What was your experience of writing "what I like about you" lists for friends or family members? Who else would you like to give this kind of list to?

7:45 to 8:30 p.m. - Presentation: Transition: four stages of rebellion, family of origin influences, childhood influences, leftovers and power struggles.

8:30 to 8:45 p.m. - Break.

8:45 to 9:00 p.m. - Discuss homework assignments for next week.

9:00 to 9:15 p.m. - Warm fuzzies for those who were missing last week.(Use whatever time necessary)

9:15 to 9:50 p.m. - Small Groups:
- What stage of Fisher's growth and development model are you in? (Page 50.)
- What stage is your former love-partner in?
- What is an example of a "should" and a "want" that you're struggling with right now?
- How has this inner-conflict been projected out onto your relationships?
- Are you clear about the difference between internal and external rebellion?
- How did your family of origin or childhood influences contribute to the ending of your love relationship?
- How have your relationships with family members been affected by the ending of your love relationship?
- What changes have taken place in you since the ending of your relationship?

9:50 to 10:00 p.m. - Big group time and closure. Time for "I feel _____" messages.

Homework For Next Week's Seminar: (* Indicates Most Important Homework)
*1. Reading assignment: Chapter 13, "Openness" in *Rebuilding*.
*2. List some of the masks you've been wearing and begin to explore whether you need to continue wearing them.
3. Find positive and constructive methods of rebellion that will improve your self-worth and help you establish your identity.
4. Identify childhood and family of origin influences that are negatively affecting your relationships.
5. Continue writing in your journal about these influences and how they are affecting your relationships.
6. For more information on family of origin, childhood influences, power struggles, and finding identity through rebellion, we suggest you read *Loving Choices*, by Bruce Fisher and Nina Hart.

Fisher's Theory of Growth and Development

It appears in our society that people mature through four stages of growth and development while attempting to gain an individual identity separate from expectations of parents and society. Part of this process is to look at the adaptive/survivor behaviors you learned in your developmental years. Below is an outline of these four stages.

Stages	Shell	External Rebellion	Internal Rebellion	Love
Ages in each stage (Ages vary a great deal)	0-10 years	10-16 years	Anytime person finds courage and strength to do it.	16 years or more
Relationship with Parents	Stable. Child pleasing parent.	Unstable. Child rebelling.	More peaceful. Less projection.	Adult-to-adult. Compassionate.
Communication	Superficial. Few arguments.	Lousy. Many contradictions.	Child accessing adaptive voices from within.	Active listening. More self disclosure.
Attitude	Tries to please. What will people think?	Pushing for limits.	Ownership and responsibility.	Acceptance. I'm okay — You're okay.
Affect	Withdrawn. Identity hidden.	Gaining freedom and emotional strength.	Gaining identity and balance within.	Secure identity. Mature ability to love.

Psychologist Haim Ginot, in his book, *Between Parent and Child*, describes three stages of growth he calls organization, disorganization, and reorganization. Oscar Wilde mentions how children start out loving their parents, then reject them, and sometimes learn to accept them. Hegel, the 18th-19th century German philosopher, talked about the stages of thesis, anti-thesis, and syn-thesis. Plato in his *The Myth of the Cave*, talked about how people go through a process of leaving the shackles in the cave to search for the truth outside of the cave.

This model looks at rebellion as a search for mature identity and a much more positive emotion than commonly believed in our society. There are two malfunctions keeping people from growing through the stages. If children in rebellion fail to receive appropriate limits, they find difficulty gaining the emotional strength needed to grow out of the shell stage. Secondly, children find it difficult to grow beyond the stage that their parents are in.

The emotional and internal pressures that a person experiences, which motivate them to start seeking their identity, are often related to being out of balance. Usually one of the adaptive/survivor parts has been "driving their personality car." For example, the "shoulds" you have been feeling result in you being over-responsible and you experience the burdens of the whole world upon your shoulders. You are attempting to rebel in order to become responsible-for-self instead of being over-responsible.

People often do an external rebellion in which they project their lack of freedom upon others around them. They perceive others are keeping them from becoming mature and free. We recommend learning to do an internal rebellion where people learn to identify their adaptive/survivor behaviors which keep them from becoming free. Internal rebellion is where the search for mature identity happens.

External rebellion places great stress upon people's close relationships, and love-relationships become stressful and often end. Internal rebellion is possible to do within the confines of a marriage or important relationship, and allows people to find individual identity while in emotionally close relationships. If the partner of the person in rebellion will make the choice to look at their adaptive/survivor parts, which are usually parental, then they may make the crisis of their partner being in rebellion, a creative experience. Internal rebellion from one person, and ownership of parental behavior in partner, will allow love relationships to survive the crisis of rebellion.

Use this page to take notes from the presentation in Session Six on the four stages of rebellion, family of origin influences, childhood influences, leftovers, and power struggles.

Affirmations

Writing and saying affirmations out loud can be a powerful experience. Here are some examples of affirmations. We invite you to write one or more affirmations that are important for you in your own personal growth and self-actualization. Post them in a prominent place and say them out loud at least once a day.

1. The more I understand myself, the better I feel.
2. I appreciate my ability to apply the things I'm learning to my every day life.

My first affirmation is:

My second affirmation is:

My third affirmation is:

My reactions to the reading assignment in *Rebuilding* are:

My reactions to the Transition session of the Rebuilding class are:

What were some of the important things I learned in Session Six?

What are some of the important changes I am making in my thinking and my actions?

Openness

"I've Been Hiding Behind a Mask"

A mask is a false face — a feeling projected to others that's different from what you're really feeling. Some masks are appropriate; others are inappropriate. Masks may protect you from the emotional pain you feel or fear, but wearing masks takes a great deal of emotional energy. Masks distance you emotionally from others, keeping you from building intimate relationships. When you remove your masks appropriately, you find intimacy rather than emotional pain.

Lesson Plan for Session Seven

Openness - I've Been Hiding Behind A Mask

Goals for Session Seven:
1. To understand how you use masks to emotionally distance others.
2. To remove at least one of your masks by sharing it with others.
3. To learn how taking off a mask increases your emotional closeness and intimacy with others.
4. To learn to use affirmations that will help you become more authentic.

Agenda for Session Seven:

6:45 to 7:00 p.m. Arrive, greet new friends, get a hug, and a cup of tea or coffee.

7:00 to 7:10 p.m. Centering and Connecting Exercise. Discuss lesson plans.

7:10 to 7:50 p.m. Discussion of masks.

7:50 to 8:30 p.m. Small Groups:
What masks do you often wear? What's under each of the masks that you're afraid to expose? (Usually, some kind of fear or pain.) Which ones are really necessary (and why)? Which ones could you let go of? Who are the people you're in growing relationships with — those you'd find it easier to take your masks off with? Why? What would happen if you took off some of your unnecessary masks? How's your self-worth these days? What could you do to improve it?

8:30 to 8:45 p.m. Break.

8:45 to 9:00 p.m. Discuss homework assignments for next week.

9:00 to 9:55 p.m. Large group Unmasking Exercise:
Each participant:
1. Share a mask you have been wearing (take off the most difficult mask you are able to).
2. Share the feeling (usually fear or pain) underneath the mask which has kept you from taking it off before. It may feel scary to be this vulnerable! Remember that in reality, this is a powerful way of getting to know yourself better, as well as becoming intimate with others. Notice how many of us have been wearing similar masks and how good it feels to be yourself.

9:55 to 10:00 p.m. Closure and time for "I feel ____" messages.

Homework For Next Week's Seminar: (* Indicates Most Important Homework)
*1. Read Chapter 14, "Love" in *Rebuilding*.
*2. Continue taking off some masks that you don't need to wear anymore.
*3. Write a definition of love as used in a love-relationship. Example, "Love is _____."
  4. What did you learn as a child, adolescent, and young adult about love?
  5. Fill out the Johari Window.

Johari Window

from *Group Process: An Introduction to Group Dynamics,* Third Edition, by Joseph Luft, Copyright © 1984, 1970, 1963 by Joseph Luft. Reprinted by permission of Mayfield Publishing Company.

Known to self and others	Known to others Not known to self
Known to self Not known to others	Unknown to self and others

Before group experience

Known to self and others	Known to others Not known to self
	Unknown to self and others
Known to self Not known to others	

After group experience

The Different Areas of Your Personality

Area 1 (upper left):
The open area refers to the part of your personality that is known to yourselves and others.

Area 2 (upper right):
The blind area refers to the part of your personality that is known to others but not to yourself.

Area 3 (lower left):
The hidden area refers to the part of your personality that is known to yourself but not to others.

Area 4 (lower right):
The unknown area refers to the part of your personality that is unknown to you and to others. You know it is there because eventually many of these areas become known and you realize these unknown areas have been influencing your behavior more than you were aware.

Principles of Change

1. A change in any area will affect all other areas.
2. It takes emotional energy to keep feelings and motivations hidden or denied.
3. Threatening feelings and situations tend to decrease openness and awareness; trusting feelings and situations tend to increase openness and awareness.
4. Forcing openness, awareness, exposure is undesirable and usually ineffective
5. Openness and free activity are helpful because more of one's resources and skills can be utilized.
6. Increasing the open area usually increases the ability to communicate meaningfully with another person.
7. There is a universal curiosity about the unknown area which often is referred to as the "dark" or "disowned" side. This curiosity is held in check by custom, social inhibitions, personal anxieties, etc.
8. We should remain sensitive to the hidden areas in ourselves and in others, and respect the desire of ourselves and others to keep the areas hidden until ready to be exposed.
9. The ten-week educational seminar helps to increase both individual and group awareness and to expand Area 1.
10. The size of the areas may change. For example, when you experience grief the open area may decrease in size until you have worked through the grief process.

Exercise

Draw a window for your present self. Draw what you would like your window to look like.

Use this page to take notes during the presentation in Session Seven on Openness and the masks that we hide behind.

Please Hear What I Am Not Saying

Don't be fooled by me. Don't be fooled by the face I wear. I wear a mask, I wear a thousand masks. Masks that I am afraid to take off — and none of these masks are me. Pretending is an art that is second nature with me. Don't be fooled, for God's sake, don't be fooled. I give you the impression that I am secure, that all is sunny and unruffled within me as well as without, that confidence is my name and coolness is my game, that the water is calm and I am in command, and that I need no one. But please don't believe me. My surface may seem smooth, but my surface is my mask, my ever varying and ever concealing mask.

*Beneath lies no smugness, no complacence. Beneath dwells the real me in confusion, in fear, in aloneness. But I hide this. I don't want anybody to know it. I panic at the thought of my weakness and my fear of being exposed. That's why I frantically create a mask to hide behind, a nonchalant, sophisticated facade to help me pretend, to shield me from the glance that knows. But such a glance is what I need. And I know it. That is, if the glance is followed by acceptance and if it's followed by **love**.*

It can help me liberate me from myself, from my own self-built prison walls, from the barriers I so painstakingly erect. It will assure me of what I can't assure myself, that I am really something. But I don't tell you this, I don't dare. I'm afraid to. I'm afraid your glance will not be followed by acceptance and love. I'm afraid you'll think less of me, that you'll laugh, discover I'm just no good and reject me. So I play my game, my desperate, pretending game with a facade of assurance without, and with a trembling child within.

*And so begins my parade of masks, the glittering, but empty parade of masks. My life becomes a front. I wildly chatter to you in the suave tones of surface talk. I tell you everything that is nothing and nothing that is everything, of what's crying inside me. So when I'm going through my routine, do not be fooled by what I'm saying. **Please listen carefully and try to hear what I am not saying. What I would like to be able to say. What for survival I need to say. But what I can't say.***

*I dislike hiding. Honestly, I dislike the surface game I am playing, the superficial phony. I'd like to be really genuine and spontaneous even when that's the last thing I seem to want or need. You can help wipe away from my eyes the blank stare of the living dead. You can help call me into **aliveness**. Each time you're kind and gentle and encouraging, each time you try to understand because you really care, my heart begins to grow wings, very small wings, very feeble wings, but wings. With your sensitivity and compassion and your power of understanding, you can breathe life into me. I want you to know that. I want you to know how important you are to me. How you help me find the real person that is inside of me if you choose to. Please choose.*

*You can help me break down the wall behind which I tremble. You can help me remove the mask. You can help release me from my lonely prison. So do not pass me by. Please don't pass me by. It will not be easy for you. My long conviction of worthlessness builds strong walls. The nearer you approach me, the blinder I might strike back. It's irrational, but despite what books say about a person, I am irrational. **I fight against the very thing I cry out for.** But I am told that love is stronger than strong walls, and in this lies my hope. My only hope. Please try to beat down my wall with firm hands, but gentle hands, for my inner child is very sensitive.*

*Who am I you may wonder? I am someone you know very well. For I am **every man and woman you meet. I am the person right in front of you!***

—Author Unknown

I Am Me
My Declaration of Self-Esteem

In all the world, there is no one else exactly like me. Everything that comes out of me is authentically mine because I alone choose it. I own everything about me, my body, my mouth, my voice, my feelings, and my actions, whether they are expressed toward others or toward me. I own my fantasies, my dreams, my hopes, my fears. I own all my triumphs and successes, all my failures and mistakes. Because I own all of me, I can become intimately acquainted with myself. In doing so I can love myself and be friendly with myself and all of the parts of me. I know there are aspects about me that puzzle me and other aspects that I do not know. But as long as I am friendly and loving toward myself, I can courageously and hopefully look for solutions to my puzzles and ways to find out more about myself. However I look and sound, whatever I say and do, and whatever I think and feel at a given moment in time is authentically me. If I find some parts of how I look, sound, think and feel turn out to be unfitting, I can discard that which is unfitting, keep the rest, and invent something new for that which I discard. I can see, hear, feel, think, say and do. I have the tools to survive, to be close to others, to be productive, and to make sense and order out of the world of people and things outside of me. I own me, and therefore I can engineer me.
I am me, and I am okay.

— Author Unknown

"Micro-Lab" Small Group Activity

The purpose of this group activity is to build group trust and ability to share and for each group member to learn to invest themselves into the group process. Questions are designed to start on a more superficial level and to delve deeper with each question. Expected time to complete will be from one to one and one-half hours. A different person starts each time when answering the next question.

Questions

1. What are appropriate masks?

2. What are inappropriate masks?

3. When does the same mask change from one to the other?

4. Does your mask keep others from knowing you, or does it keep you from knowing yourself?

Affirmations

Writing and saying affirmations out loud can be a powerful experience. Here are some examples of affirmations. We invite you to write one or more affirmations that are important for you in your own personal growth and self-actualization. Post them in a prominent place and say them out loud at least once a day.

1. I can share with certain others what I am feeling and thinking without being afraid.
2. I'd rather be authentic than carry the weight of a mask.

My first affirmation is:

My second affirmation is:

My third affirmation is:

My reactions to the reading assignment in *Rebuilding* are:

My reactions to the Openness session of the Rebuilding class are:

What were some of the important things I learned in Session Seven?

What are some of the important changes I am making in my thinking and my actions?

Journal (See note on page 6.)

Session Eight
Love

"Could Somebody Really Care for Me?"

Many people need to relearn how to love, in order to love more maturely. Your capacity to love others is closely related to your capacity to love yourself. And learning to love yourself is not selfish and conceited. In fact, it is the most mentally healthy thing you can do. There are a number of specific steps you can take to increase your self-love.

Lesson Plan for Session Eight
Love: Could Somebody Really Care for Me?

Goals for Session Eight:
1. To learn more about loving yourself.
2. To gain a better understanding of ways you can be more loving to others.
3. To learn that your capacity to love others (and to receive love from them) is closely related to your ability to love yourself.
4. To learn about some different styles of loving such as friendship, romantic, altruistic, game playing, possessive, practical.
5. To learn and use affirmations that will help you develop more love for yourself and others.
6. To touch on the need for boundaries in all your relationships, especially the closest ones.

Agenda for Session Eight:

6:45 to 7:00 p.m. Arrive, greet new friends, get a hug, and a cup of tea or coffee.

7:00 to 7:10 p.m. Centering and Connecting Exercise.

7:10 to 7:45 p.m. Share your definition of love with the group.

7:45 to 8:30 p.m. Large group discussion of Chapter 14, "Love."

8:30 to 8:45 p.m. Break.

8:45 to 9:00 p.m. Discuss the homework assignments for next week. Verify correct names, addresses and phone numbers for final class list.

9:00 to 9:55 p.m. Small group discussion:
- Describe your personal growth since the crisis that led you here began.
- What can you do that will help you to love and accept yourself more?
- How do you express your love? How would you like to be loved by others?
- How did your parents or primary caretakers express self-love?
- How did your parents/caretakers express love for each other?
- What is your primary style of loving? (See pages 182-185 in *Rebuilding*.)
- What was your primary style of loving in your last love relationship?
- How did it change over time during the relationship?
- What style(s) of loving would you like to be a part of your next love relationship?

9:55 to 10:00 p.m. Closure. Time for "I feel ____" messages.

Homework For Next Week's Seminar: (* Indicates Most Important Homework)
*1. Read Chapter 16, "Relatedness" in *Rebuilding*.
*2. List the people you're in important growing relationships with and make some notes about the things you're learning from each of them.
3. Suggested topics to journal about or explore:
   Is there a balance between the love I'm giving and receiving?
   When I say, "I love you" to someone, what am I expecting to receive?
   How full is my cup? What do I need to do for myself to fill it up?
4. Read Chapter 15, "Trust" in *Rebuilding*.

What Do You Know About Love?

1. How do you know you are lovable?

2. What makes you afraid of being loved?

3. What makes you afraid of loving another?

4. What is love? How do you live it?

5. How do you express your love? How would you like to be loved?

6. How are you able to meet your own needs without feeling selfish?

7. What makes it possible for you to accept love from others?

8. How do others know you love them?

9. How do you love yourself?

10. Describe your personal growth since the crisis that led you here began.

11. How is your love becoming more mature? In what ways is your love immature?
    How is/was your love needy? How is/was your love overly dependent?

What we do not have, we cannot give. To love another, we must first love ourselves. Still, there persists the idea that to love oneself is an egocentric, infantile, destructive notion. Simple logic tells us that we can only give what we possess and that the more we possess, the greater our capacity to give. If you truly love someone, it follows that you want that person to have the best you have to offer, for the other's sake as well as yours. It is through an understanding and acceptance of yourself, your needs and what you require for happiness that you can comprehend and appreciate the needs of others. Love has acquired its tenuous reputation because for so long it has been left in the hands of amateurs who distrust it and themselves.

Use this page to take notes from the presentation in Session Eight on Love.

Love

Love, they said,
Is a passionate
Terrible thing.
A thing painfully exciting
And full of tortures.
This, they said,
Is love.

And so I thought…
Then, I loved… and was loved.
And then I knew.

Love, I say,
Is a gentle
Sacred thing.
A smile, caress, a look,
The holy touch of God.
This, I say,
Is love.

And so I know.

—JoAnn

♥♥♥♥♥♥♥♥♥♥♥♥♥

You are your own best friend, and worst enemy.
As you think, so shall it be.
All the events in your life are there because you drew them there;
what you choose to do with them is up to you.
Argue for your limitations and sure enough — they're yours.
You are beautiful — inside and out!!
Give to yourself what you give to others.
When you stop needing to be loved so much,
And it dawns on you that you are the only person who can fill the void,
Perhaps true freedom will prevail.
It doesn't matter what other people think about you,
It only matters what you think about you,
And as you think, so it is!

—Bruce

Happiness — It's Only Natural

Once you see these factors as simply the unchangeable realities of your earlier life, rather than problems, you can put the responsibility for change where it belongs; on you today, and not on your background. How to go about it? Here are seven suggestions that should help.

1. Eliminate all *roles* that you've adopted in your life; behave as you want to rather than in terms of how you feel you're *supposed* to. If your behavior has been circumscribed by a role, then you as a person have been negated, and the role has taken over. There is no "right" way for people to behave. Be *you* each moment and rid yourself of roles.

2. Take constructive risks in your life. If you've always been shy and reserved, introduce yourself to a stranger. If you want to tell your mother how you feel about her behavior, do it. Most risks involve no personal danger, only anxiety. And you will find that the more you muster the courage to do the things you truly want for yourself, however risky, the more effective you will become at living happily.

3. Eliminate all blame sentences from your vocabulary. Stop saying, "*They're* to blame" for *your* unhappiness. Replace blame sentences, such as "she made me feel bad when I heard what she said."

4. Be assertive. You are an adult, responsible for your own life. You never need ask anyone how you ought to lead that life. While you may want to see how your behavior will affect people, that doesn't mean you must seek their permission.

5. Several times a day, stop thinking and analyzing, and let your brain slip into neutral. Take a minute to concentrate on a color, pushing out all other thoughts. Or take a walk, with your thoughts "free-wheeling." Just as the body needs rest and exercise periods, so does the mind.

6. Stop looking outside yourself for validation of your worth, beauty, intellect, and personality. When you fish for compliments, ask yourself if *you* are satisfied with your performance or looks. If so, ask yourself why you need anyone else to say so. You'll discover that the less approval you seek, the more you will receive.

7. Decide to appreciate life even when "nay-sayers" and grumps are determined to drag you down. Surround yourself with happy faces. Stop feeling it is *your* responsibility to change those who insist on being unhappy.

   Your own expectations are the key to this whole business of mental health. If you expect to be happy, healthy and fulfilled in life, then most likely it will work out that way.

— Author Unknown

Affirmations

Writing and saying affirmations out loud can be a powerful experience. Following are some examples of affirmations. We invite you to write one or more affirmations of the affirmations that are important for you in your own personal growth and self-actualization. Post them in a prominent place and say them out loud at least once a day.

1. I am loving myself more and more each day.
2. I am giving myself the love I deserve to receive from myself and others.

My first affirmation is:

My second affirmation is:

My third affirmation is:

My reactions to the reading assignment in *Rebuilding* are:

My reactions to the Love session of the Rebuilding class are:

What were some of the important things I learned in Session Eight?

What are some of the important changes I am making in my thinking and my actions?

Session Nine
Relatedness
"Growing Relationships Help Me Rebuild"

It's okay to have an important relationship after your primary relationship has ended. We often need support, companionship, and feedback from others to help us rebuild. These relationships are often short-term, so we need to learn how to have "healthy termination." We need to take credit for creating these relationships as part of our growing process. And we need to become aware of how we can make these relationships as growing and healing as possible.

Lesson Plan for Session Nine

Relatedness: Growing Relationships Help Me Rebuild

Goals for Session Nine:

1. To understand how growing relationships can be a part of your personal growth process.
2. To understand the need for nurturing that can be a part of growing relationships.
3. To help you feel empowered to make necessary choices and to be yourself in your relationships.
4. To understand that growing relationships can happen with all kinds of people, such as other seminar members, friends, family, therapists, clergy, as well as love partners.
5. To understand ways of helping growing relationships to become long term relationships when appropriate, but they don't have to become long-term in order for you to grow and benefit from them.
6. To understand the difference between a *growing* relationship and a "running-from-knowing-myself/avoiding-loneliness" *rebound* relationship.
7. To give yourself permission to take some relationship risks and go out and "get your nose bloodied" (in other words, experiment with growing relationships).
8. To learn that some relationships just don't work for you or are toxic or destructive and need to end, and to learn about "healthy terminations."
9. To learn and use affirmations that will help you take more responsibility for your relationships.

Agenda for Session Nine:

6:45 to 7:00 p.m. Arrive, greet new friends, get a hug, and a cup of tea or coffee.

7:00 to 7:30 p.m. Complete and turn in the second *Fisher Divorce Adjustment Scale*.

7:30 to 8:30 p.m. Presentation and discussion of "Growing Relationships."

8:30 to 8:45 p.m. Break.

8:45 to 9:05 p.m. Large group sharing:
List the characteristics of an ideal love relationship. List hopes and fears about relationships.

9:05 to 9:50 p.m. Small or large group discussion:
- What kinds of improvements do you need to make in your relationship with yourself?
- What are the relationship skills you need to learn and/or practice?
  (Examples: communication, feeling expression, boundaries, ownership, trust, vulnerability, honesty, etc.)
- What kind of growing relationships would be helpful for you at this point in your process?
- If you can't imagine having another love-relationship in the future, what would you need to do before you would be ready to have one?
- What are your hopes and fears about dating?
- What can you do to reduce your fears? What can you do to make your hopes a reality?

9:50 to 10:00 p.m. Closure. Time for "I feel ____" messages.

Homework For Next Week's Seminar: (* Indicates Most Important Homework)
*1. Reading Assignment: Chapter 17 "Sexuality" and Chapter 19, "Purpose."
*2. Make a list of sexuality questions. These will be asked anonymously of participants next week in a group discussion.
3. Extra-credit homework: Complete your lifeline. See example on page 246 of *Rebuilding*.
4. Practice using "I" messages as described on Page 211 of *Rebuilding*. This is the most important single behavior you can do to improve your communication skills!
5. If possible, read Chapter 18, "Singleness" in *Rebuilding*.
   Many facilitators and seminar groups like to begin Session Ten with a potluck party. If this class plans to do so, we will start eating about 6:30 p.m. (Suggestion: Bring paper plates and silverware.)

Today

Today was my day.
Once more God looked on me,
And blessed me,
And laughed with me.
Today.

Now I know the confidence
of strength,
I was afraid,
There is no fear.
I was hurt,
And the pain is gone.
Today.

Where are the trumpets?
Call them out!
Blow them loud . . .
For today was my day.

I cried,
And hurt,
And loved,
And lived.

Today
My cup runneth over.
What then of tomorrow?

—JoAnn

Growing Relationships

Just what is a "growing relationship" anyway? Here are some of the ingredients that I believe are important.

- It has good communication, using "I" messages rather than "you" messages.
- With obstacles and problems, you are committed to talking it out rather than acting it out.
- You take ownership for what you are creating in your life.
- There is a comfortable amount of being vulnerable — not too little, nor too much.
- There is dedication towards growing and learning about yourself.
- There is a commitment to embracing your pain and learning from it.
- There is a balance between giving and taking, between being responsible and having fun.
- There is a balance between following tradition and a willingness to try new things.
- There are flexible boundaries instead of walls.
- You are able to do self-care without feeling selfish.
- You are more inner-directed than other-directed.
- You live more in the present than the past or the future.
- You are committed to being you rather than looking for a committed relationship.
- You invest equally in your physical, emotional, social, and spiritual growth.
- You are dedicated to taming your adaptive/survivor parts instead letting them control your behavior.
- It can be with a therapist, friend, family member, relative, or a love relationship with the above traits.

Have you realized one of the most important things you have learned in the Rebuilding Seminar? You have been practicing and creating these growing relationships with the other class participants. Your challenge is easily defined. Keep on creating the same kind of growing and healthy relationships that you have experienced in the Rebuilding Seminar for the rest of your life. It may be one of the most valuable lessons you have learned in this class!

— Bruce

Use this page to take notes from the presentation in Session Nine on Relatedness.

Listening is Loving

What is active listening?

Listening actively rather than passively.

Participatory: you give feedback and respond.

Letting the other person know that you heard.

What does it do?

Facilitates communication.

Makes the other person feel important.

Provides a place to air feelings and thoughts, non-threateningly.

Allows and encourages expression of thoughts and feelings.

Provides an atmosphere for each person to see what he or she has expressed more objectively.

Affirms the value of the other person and his or her ideas, attitudes, feelings.

Creates an equal relationship between two people, rather than, "I know more than you."

Effective Listening

(From Alberti and Emmons, *Your Perfect Right*, reprinted with permission of the publisher.)

Assertive listening involves an active commitment to the other person. It requires your full attention, and calls for no overt act on your part, although eye contact and certain gestures — such as nodding — are often appropriate. Listening demonstrates your respect for the other person. It requires that you avoid expressing *yourself* for a time, yet is not a nonassertive act.

Listening is not simply the physical response of hearing sounds — indeed, deaf persons may be excellent "listeners." Effective listening may involve giving feedback to the other person, so that it is clear that you understood what was said. Assertive listening requires at least these elements:

- *tuning in* to the other person, by stopping other activities, turning off the TV, ignoring other distractions, focusing your energy in his or her direction;
- *attending* to the message, by making eye contact if possible, nodding to show that you hear, perhaps touching her or him; and
- actively attempting to *understand* before responding, by thinking about the underlying message — the feelings behind the words — rather than trying to interpret, or to come up with an answer.

Attending Skills

(Adapted from Ivey, *The Skilled Helper*, reprinted with permission of the publisher.)

Ask open-ended questions.

Avoid yes-or-no questions.

Avoid "why" questions which block communication.

Use "what" and "how."

Use minimal encouragement:

- Nodding of head, eye contact
- "Uh-huh"
- "Yes"
- "Go on"
- "And"
- "Because"

Avoid rescuing.

Allow other person to have pain, confusion, sadness, and anger as part of their learning.

Nurture without bleeding with them; keep objective.

Believe that people can solve their problems if given a chance to talk in a non-threatening situation.

Questions for Discussion

1. What is required to trust members of the opposite sex?

2. How are men and women alike in their responses to feelings such as love, hate, intimacy and fear?

3. How are men and women different in their responses to feelings such as love, hate, intimacy and fear?

4. How do I know that I can trust myself and my feelings?

5. What feelings do I trust in myself and act upon?

6. What makes it possible to become emotionally close to a potential love-partner?

7. How do I distance myself from other people? How do I keep other people away?

8. What relationships am I building that help me heal my love wound? Why is this important?

9. What am I doing to build healing and trusting relationships with friends of both sexes?

10. What happens when I give mixed messages rather than communicate my real feelings?

11. How do I know when I can't trust another person?

12. How do I know when I can trust another person?

13. Why is it important to heal my love-wound? How will healing my love-wound help me experience intimacy?

14. What does it mean to live in the present in my relationships?

15. What is the primary difference between engaging in a short-term relationship versus a long-term relationship?

16. What kinds of risks am I taking in my relationship besides exposing my true feelings and thoughts?

17. How do I express true interest in my friends? How is that different from looking for another love relationship?

Affirmations

Writing and saying affirmations out loud can be a powerful experience. Here are some examples of affirmations. We invite you to write one or more affirmations that are important for you in your own personal growth and self-actualization. Post them in a prominent place and say them out loud at least once a day.

1. I can trust myself, and be myself in all my relationships.
2. I feel more internal peace when I connect with myself and others honestly and openly, with boundaries and with love.

My first affirmation is:

My second affirmation is:

My third affirmation is:

My reactions to the reading assignment in *Rebuilding* are:

My reactions to the Openness session of the Rebuilding class are:

What were some of the important things I learned in Session Nine?

What are some of the important changes I am making in my thinking and my actions?

Journal (See note on page 6.)

Session Ten
Sexuality

"I'm Interested, But I'm Scared"

When you're first separated, it's normal to be extremely fearful of sex. During the adjustment process, you can learn to express your unique sexuality according to your own moral standards. The singles subculture emphasizes authenticity, responsibility, and individuality more than rules. You can discover what you believe rather than what is expected of you. The great difference in attitudes and values of male and female sexuality appears to be a myth. Your adjustment may be complicated by the major changes taking place in female and male sex roles. In any case, safe sex is the order of the day.

Lesson Plan for Session Ten
Sexuality: I'm Interested But I'm Scared

Goals for Session Ten:
1 To become comfortable with your own sexuality.
2. To feel more comfortable talking with others about sexuality.
3. To recognize that your questions and concerns about sex and sexuality are similar to those of the opposite sex.
4. To feel empowered to live your life to the fullest and to become the person you've always wanted to be.
5. To learn and use affirmations that will help you better appreciate the beauty of your sexuality.
6. To reflect on the things you've learned and the ways you've grown in the last ten weeks.

Agenda for Session Ten:

6:30 to 7:30 p.m. Arrive, greet new friends, get a hug. If a potluck has been planned,begin eating as soon as enough food has arrived. **Celebrate and enjoy!**

7:30 to 8:30 p.m. Large group:
Fill out seminar evaluations and recommend future volunteer helpers.
Complete sexuality questionnaire, and write out your favorite sexual fantasy.
Facilitator reads the sexuality questions. Those who choose to may read the answers they wrote.
Turn the seminar evaluations and sexuality questionnaires in to the facilitator.
Pass out "graduation diplomas" and *FDAS* post-test scores.

8:30 to 9:00 p.m. Break.

9:00 to 9:20 p.m. Small groups: (Men and women in separate groups)
(Choose one person in each group who writes quickly and legibly to list the questions, ideally someone with a strong voice who will be asking them in the following large group exercise.)
Suggestion: Get started writing questions right away!!
Write down as many questions as possible that you'd like to ask the opposite sex.
List pet peeves about behaviors of the opposite sex (allow at least five minutes at the end to do this).
Questions and pet peeves will be kept anonymous!

9:20 to 10:30 p.m. Large group: Alternating after each question, the men who choose to will answer the women's' questions and then the women who choose to will answer the men's' questions. Make every effort to offer answers one at a time so all can hear. We'd like to hear some answers from everyone, but no one will be made to talk if they don't choose to. (Writers: remember to list the pet peeves as well). From time to time the facilitator will read a sexual fantasy from the sexuality questionnaires.

10:30 p.m. Closure. Time for "I feel ____" messages.

10:30 to ? Continue large group with men and women answering questions, addressing pet peeves, from the lists drawn up by the opposite sex.

Homework for the Rest of Your Life:
Love yourself!
Be your own best friend!
Feel your feelings and listen to your heart!
Tell the truth as lovingly as possible and don't be attached to the outcome!
Build strong and healthy friendships where you can give and receive love and be comfortable being yourself!

Sexuality Questionnaire

Please complete the following questions about sex:

When I think about sex I _____

_____

When I was a child I thought sex was _____

_____

Now I believe sex is _____

_____

When it came to sex my father always said _____

_____

When it came to sex my mother always said _____

_____

I grew up thinking that sexual pleasure was _____

_____

When I first started my last love relationship I expected sex to be _____

_____

From my former love-partner I got the sexual message that _____

_____

My contribution to the sexual problems in my last love relationship was _____

_____

Since my last love relationship ended sex has _____

_____

In my next love relationship (as far as sex) I'll be sure to _____

_____

My favorite sexual fantasy is _____

_____

Use this page to take notes from the presentation in Session Ten on Sexuality.

Affirmations

Writing and saying affirmations out loud can be a powerful experience. Here are some examples of affirmations. We invite you to write one or more affirmations that are important for you in your own personal growth and self-actualization. Post them in a prominent place and say them out loud at least once a day.

1. I am making loving choices in my life.
2. I am taking charge of the way I live my life.
3. I am able to build and create healthy relationships with friends of both sexes.
4. The more I get to know myself, the better I like myself.

My first affirmation is:

My second affirmation is:

My third affirmation is:

My reactions to the reading assignment in *Rebuilding* are:

My reactions to the Openness session of the Rebuilding Seminar are:

What were some of the important things I learned in Session Ten?

What are some of the important changes I am making in my thinking and my actions?

Journal (See note on page 6.)

Appendix A
Fisher Divorce Adjustment Scale

The following statements are feelings and attitudes that people frequently experience while they are ending a love relationship. Keeping in mind one specific relationship you have ended or are ending, read each statement and decide how frequently the statement applies to your present feelings and attitudes. Mark your response on your answer sheet. Do not leave any statements blank on the answer sheet. If the statement is not appropriate for you in your present situation, answer the way you feel you might if that statement were appropriate.

The five responses to choose from on the answer sheet are:

(1) almost always   **(2)** usually   **(3)** sometimes   **(4)** seldom   **(5)** almost never

1. I am comfortable telling people I am separated from my love partner.
2. I am physically and emotionally exhausted from morning until night.
3. I am constantly thinking of my former love partner.
4. I feel rejected by many of the friends I had when I was in the love relationship.
5. I become upset when I think about my former love partner.
6. I like being the person I am.
7. I feel like crying because I feel so sad.
8. I can communicate with my former love partner in a calm and rational manner.
9. There are many things about my personality I would like to change.
10. It is easy for me to accept my becoming a single person.
11. I feel depressed.
12. I feel emotionally separated from my former love partner.
13. People would not like me if they got to know me.
14. I feel comfortable seeing and talking to my former love partner.
15. I feel like I am an attractive person.
16. I feel as though I am in a daze and the world doesn't seem real.
17. I find myself doing things just to please my former love partner.
18. I feel lonely.
19. There are many things about my body I would like to change.
20. I have many plans and goals for the future.
21. I feel I don't have much sex appeal.
22. I am relating and interacting in many new ways with people since my separation.
23. Joining a singles' group would make me feel I was a loser like them.
24. It is easy for me to organize my daily routine of living.
25. I find myself making excuses to see and talk to my former love partner.
26. Because my love relationship failed, I must be a failure.
27. I feel like unloading my feelings of anger and hurt upon my former love partner.
28. I feel comfortable being with people.
29. I have trouble concentrating.
30. I think of my former love partner as related to me rather than as a separate person.

85

31. I feel like an okay person.

32. I hope my former love partner is feeling as much or more emotional pain than I am

33. I have close friends who know and understand me.

34. I am unable to control my emotions.

35. I feel capable of building a deep and meaningful love relationship.

36. I have trouble sleeping.

37. I easily become angry at my former love partner.

38. I am afraid to trust people who might become love partners.

39. Because my love relationship ended, I feel there must be something wrong with me.

40. I either have no appetite or eat continuously which is unusual for me.

41. I don't want to accept the fact that our love relationship is ending.

42. I force myself to eat even though I'm not hungry.

43. I have given up on my former love partner and I getting back together.

44. I feel very frightened inside.

45. It is important that my family, friends, and associates be on my side rather than on my former love partner's side.

46. I feel uncomfortable even thinking about dating.

47. I feel capable of living the kind of life I would like to live.

48. I have noticed my body weight is changing a great deal.

49. I believe if we try, my love partner and I can save our love relationship.

50. My abdomen feels empty and hollow.

51. I have feelings of romantic love for my former love partner.

52. I can make the decisions I need to because I know and trust my feelings.

53. I would like to get even with my former love partner for hurting me.

54. I avoid people even though I want and need friends.

55. I have really made a mess of my life.

56. I sigh a lot.

57. I believe it is best for all concerned to have our love relationship end.

58. I perform my daily activities in a mechanical and unfeeling manner.

59. I become upset when I think about my love partner having a love relationship with someone else.

60. I feel capable of facing and dealing with my problems.

61. I blame my former love partner for the failure of our love relationship.

62. I am afraid of becoming sexually involved with another person.

63. I feel adequate as a fe/male love partner.

64. It will only be a matter of time until my love partner and I get back together.

65. I feel detached and removed from activities around me as though I were watching them on a movie screen.

66. I would like to continue having a sexual relationship with my former love partner.

67. Life is somehow passing me by.

68. I feel comfortable going by myself to a public place such as a movie.

69. It is good to feel alive again after having felt numb and emotionally dead.

70. I feel I know and understand myself.

71. I feel emotionally committed to my former love partner.

72. I want to be with people but I feel emotionally distant from them.

73. I am the type of person I would like to have for a friend.

74. I am afraid of becoming emotionally close to another love partner.

75. Even on the days when I am feeling good, I may suddenly become sad and start crying.

76. I can't believe our love relationship is ending.

77. I become upset when I think about my love partner dating someone else.

78. I have a normal amount of self-confidence.

79. People seem to enjoy being with me.

80. Morally and spiritually, I believe it is wrong for our love relationship to end.

81. I wake up in the morning feeling there is no good reason to get out of bed.

82. I find myself daydreaming about all the good times I had with my love partner.

83. People want to have a love realtionship with me because I feel like a lovable person.

84. I want to hurt my former love partner by letting him/her know how much I hurt emotionally.

85. I feel comfortable going to social events even though I am single.

86. I feel guilty about my love relationship ending.

87. I feel emotionally insecure.

88. I feel uncomfortable even thinking about having a sexual relationship.

89. I feel emotionally weak and helpless.

90. I think about ending my life with suicide.

91. I understand the reasons why our love relationship did not work out.

92. I feel comfortable having my friends know our love relationship is ending.

93. I am angry about the things my former love partner has been doing.

94. I feel like I am going crazy.

95. I am unable to perform sexually.

96. I feel as though I am the only single person in a couples-only society.

97. I feel like a single person rather than a married person.

98. I feel my friends look at me as unstable now that I'm separated.

99. I daydream about being with and talking to my former love partner.

100. I need to improve my feelings of self-worth about being a wo/man.

Fisher Divorce Adjustment Scale Answer Sheet

First name _____   Last name _____

Address _____   City _____   State _____   Zip _____

Home phone _____   Work phone _____   Date _____

I am ___ male ___ female.   I am _____ years old   I have been separated _____ months

Who decided to end my relationship? ___ I did ___ my spouse did ___ both of us did ___ widowed

Please fill in the following circles to answer the questions on the *Fisher Divorce Adjustment Scale*. The five responses to choose from are:

(1) almost always   **(2)** usually   **(3)** sometimes   **(4)** seldom   **(5)** almost never

	1 2 3 4 5		1 2 3 4 5		1 2 3 4 5		1 2 3 4 5
1.	0 0 0 0 0	26.	0 0 0 0 0	51.	0 0 0 0 0	76.	0 0 0 0 0
2.	0 0 0 0 0	27.	0 0 0 0 0	52.	0 0 0 0 0	77.	0 0 0 0 0
3.	0 0 0 0 0	28.	0 0 0 0 0	53.	0 0 0 0 0	78.	0 0 0 0 0
4.	0 0 0 0 0	29.	0 0 0 0 0	54.	0 0 0 0 0	79.	0 0 0 0 0
5.	0 0 0 0 0	30.	0 0 0 0 0	55.	0 0 0 0 0	80.	0 0 0 0 0
6.	0 0 0 0 0	31.	0 0 0 0 0	56.	0 0 0 0 0	81.	0 0 0 0 0
7.	0 0 0 0 0	32.	0 0 0 0 0	57.	0 0 0 0 0	82.	0 0 0 0 0
8.	0 0 0 0 0	33.	0 0 0 0 0	58.	0 0 0 0 0	83.	0 0 0 0 0
9.	0 0 0 0 0	34.	0 0 0 0 0	59.	0 0 0 0 0	84.	0 0 0 0 0
10.	0 0 0 0 0	35.	0 0 0 0 0	60.	0 0 0 0 0	85.	0 0 0 0 0
11.	0 0 0 0 0	36.	0 0 0 0 0	61.	0 0 0 0 0	86.	0 0 0 0 0
12.	0 0 0 0 0	37.	0 0 0 0 0	62.	0 0 0 0 0	87.	0 0 0 0 0
13.	0 0 0 0 0	38.	0 0 0 0 0	63.	0 0 0 0 0	88.	0 0 0 0 0
14.	0 0 0 0 0	39.	0 0 0 0 0	64.	0 0 0 0 0	89.	0 0 0 0 0
15.	0 0 0 0 0	40.	0 0 0 0 0	65.	0 0 0 0 0	90.	0 0 0 0 0
16.	0 0 0 0 0	41.	0 0 0 0 0	66.	0 0 0 0 0	91.	0 0 0 0 0
17.	0 0 0 0 0	42.	0 0 0 0 0	67.	0 0 0 0 0	92.	0 0 0 0 0
18.	0 0 0 0 0	43.	0 0 0 0 0	68.	0 0 0 0 0	93.	0 0 0 0 0
19.	0 0 0 0 0	44.	0 0 0 0 0	69.	0 0 0 0 0	94.	0 0 0 0 0
20.	0 0 0 0 0	45.	0 0 0 0 0	70.	0 0 0 0 0	95.	0 0 0 0 0
21.	0 0 0 0 0	46.	0 0 0 0 0	71.	0 0 0 0 0	96.	0 0 0 0 0
22.	0 0 0 0 0	47.	0 0 0 0 0	72.	0 0 0 0 0	97.	0 0 0 0 0
23.	0 0 0 0 0	48.	0 0 0 0 0	73.	0 0 0 0 0	98.	0 0 0 0 0
24.	0 0 0 0 0	49.	0 0 0 0 0	74.	0 0 0 0 0	99.	0 0 0 0 0
25.	0 0 0 0 0	50.	0 0 0 0 0	75.	0 0 0 0 0	100.	0 0 0 0 0

Note: If you copy this answer sheet on a copy machine, make sure the copy is exactly the same spacing as the original if you want to hand score the answers using the transparencies.

Appendix B
Rebuilding Seminar Final Course Evaluation

Please rate the following areas of the Fisher Rebuilding Seminar by circling the appropriate number. The higher the number, the more valuable and worthwhile you found that activity or evening to be. If you cannot evaluate a particular area, please circle "NA" for "Not able."

Class Sessions	Least to Most Worthwhile
Session 1: Rebuilding Blocks	1 2 3 4 5 NA
Session 2: Adaptation	1 2 3 4 5 NA
Session 3: Grief	1 2 3 4 5 NA
Session 4: Anger	1 2 3 4 5 NA
Session 5: Self-worth	1 2 3 4 5 NA
Session 6: Transition	1 2 3 4 5 NA
Session 7: Openness	1 2 3 4 5 NA
Session 8: Love	1 2 3 4 5 NA
Session 9: Relatedness	1 2 3 4 5 NA
Session 10: Sexuality	1 2 3 4 5 NA
Taking the *Fisher Divorce Adjustment Scale*	1 2 3 4 5 NA
Textbook *Rebuilding*	1 2 3 4 5 NA
Parties and activities outside of class	1 2 3 4 5 NA
Large group discussions	1 2 3 4 5 NA
Small group discussions	1 2 3 4 5 NA
Friendships you made during the class	1 2 3 4 5 NA
Huggles	1 2 3 4 5 NA
Volunteers	1 2 3 4 5 NA
Books and outside reading other than textbook	1 2 3 4 5 NA
Homework assignments	1 2 3 4 5 NA
Total class experience	1 2 3 4 5 NA

What did you like best about the class?

What did you like least about the class?

What would you like to see added in the future?

Selection Of New Volunteers
The selection process for volunteers is: (1) voting by other class members, (2) feedback from the present volunteers, (3) decision by facilitator, (4) discussion between facilitator and prospective volunteer, and (5) attending the volunteer training workshop.
Please nominate people in the class who you think would be good volunteers in future classes.

Appendix C
Rebuilding Blocks for Widows and Widowers
The following pages are a substitution for Chapter One in the *Rebuilding* textbook.

The purpose of this section is to provide some understanding into the unique issues effecting the widowed. The rebuilding concepts are translated into a language that fits better for widowed people.

Dumper and Dumpee for the Widowed

You may be saying or at least thinking, "What does dumper or dumpee have to do with me? I am widowed."

At first glance these terms do not seem to apply. The person you loved did not leave the relationship to continue with his or her life. Your love-partner left the relationship in one of two ways: Through sudden death or lingering illness. Remember that dumpers are those who begin to grieve before the end of the relationship. Dumpees begin the grieving when the relationship ends. Using these definitions it is possible to apply the terms to yourself.

A widow or widower whose spouse died quickly is forced to begin the grieving process and can feel emotionally numb at first. The full impact of what has happened is often not felt until after the funeral. In one sense, the widowed have been dumped on. That person did not choose the relationship's end. Therefore, the surviving spouse is similar to the dumpee in a divorce, experiencing many of the same thoughts and feelings, because the death occurred suddenly.

However, when the death is slow, its course over a period of time, the surviving spouse may experience more thoughts and feelings parallel to the dumper. Widows whose spouses die after a prolonged illness will be more likely to start the grieving process before the death of their loved one. They may react to the death of their spouse with relief. They will often appear to be coping well, but also have had more time to react to the situation because they started grieving at a different point in the relationship.

It is also possible you will have some combination of dumper and dumpee thoughts and feelings. You may not precisely fit into one of the categories. What is important is that you become aware of, and acknowledge, how you are experiencing your spouse's death. You may have conflicting feelings regarding how being widowed will impact your life. You may have some underlying judgments regarding those feelings which hinder you from fully embracing what you are experiencing.

The following is an attempt to translate the rebuilding blocks into a more meaningful exploration of the issues directly impacting your life.

Denial

Denial is an emotional safety valve. When faced with something physically painful the body will try to compensate, and in severe pain, will cause unconsciousness. Emotions can respond to pain in a similar way.

For dumpees, denial is reflected in statements like: "This can't be happening to me," "This is a sick joke, it can't be true." In extreme cases denial may include clinging to the delusion that the spouse will return. You may have said to yourself, "When I go home today my wife will be in the kitchen like she always is cooking dinner", or "If I just wait long enough he'll be back."

Dumpers also experience denial, but usually before the actual death. Denial for you occurs when you first hear the news that your spouse is dying. "He isn't really dying," or "Medicine will find a cure," are statements which may indicate denial. It may be difficult to distinguish between denial and hope. However, an unwillingness to even acknowledge the possibility of death is a strong sign you may be struggling with denial. The important thing to remember about this stage is that it occurs very strongly at first and does not fade entirely until the grieving process is well underway.

Fear

This may be your most predominant emotion. It is one of the reasons for denial; facing the fears seems like too much to bear. There are two primary categories of fears you may experience: 1) Fear of dying, and 2) Fear of living. When your spouse died you came closer than ever to your own mortality. Many people avoid facing the prospect that death is inevitable. When your spouse died your own underlying fear that you too will die may have surfaced. This is especially true if your spouse died suddenly. You may also fear dying because your spouse is no longer available to meet your needs or take care of you. Many were totally dependent in some way upon their spouses. "What's going to happen to me now?" is a common fear.

The fear of living may take on any of a number of faces. You may fear all the lifestyle adjustments and new choices. You may fear your own feelings and thoughts related to your spouse's death, especially if you experienced some relief- which is likely to be true when death occurs over a period of time.

Adaptation

We live in a couple's world. None of us planned that when we pledged, "till death do us part," we would actually see the end of our marriage. Oh, we knew that we would not live forever, but we never consciously thought that our spouse would die. Well, yours did, and here you are, still alive, left to make a thousand adjustments. The first one being dealing with the fact you are single.

You may resist accepting the fact that you are single. What if someone asks you out on a date. That would be absolutely terrifying. All the dynamics of potentially starting a new relationship may seem so complicated. Stepping into the unknown of meeting another person is one of the major adjustments of being widowed. The longer the marriage the more difficult this prospect may be. You may cling to an image of your love-partner, and may have an even more idealized image now that your partner is dead.

It may sound cruel, but the death of your spouse is an opportunity for self-examination. How do you view yourself, life, and others? In which areas have you fallen into a rut or become stagnant? The death of your spouse is a way for you to examine any places where you have taken life for granted.

This time is also an opportunity to consider why you got married in the first place. Did you experience a successful, full, interactive relationship? Were you satisfied with the nature and dynamics of the relationship. As you adjust to singleness, introspection is an option for increasing present awareness, and future freedom.

Loneliness

You may be feeling the loneliest you've ever felt. It's painful to live with the knowledge that our spouse is not going to laugh at our jokes, or be there for us when we cry. You may have had a time apart before, such as a vacation, business trip, or hospitalization, but not have experienced this depth of loneliness. Now that the relationship has permanently ended, the other person is no longer there, and you feel totally alone.

That loneliness is magnified by the question, "Am I going to be lonely like this forever?" You begin to wonder if you'll ever have the companionship of a love-relationship again. Even with the comfort and encouragement of children or friends, this feeling can be overwhelming.

You may have felt lonely while in the relationship, especially if your spouse was in the hospital or diagnosed with a terminal illness. That form of loneliness is a special kind of pain, and the death of your spouse may actually ease some of that burden.

Socially, you might isolate yourself. You feel like the third wheel on a bicycle — not really fitting in— not needed. You can imagine that everyone is talking about you, while privately you wonder who really cares about your pain. When someone asks you about your dead spouse you don't know whether to be offended, cry, or just walk away.

You may even try to escape the feelings of loneliness by being in a crowd or constantly having people around you, while still feeling lonely. You may seek relief by becoming super busy, doing anything to escape being home alone. You may find people to go out with just to keep from being alone, even if you don't enjoy the other person's company. Sometimes anything is better than being home alone with all those feelings and memories.

As time goes on you will move beyond loneliness into accepting your *aloneness.* Aloneness is the process of becoming comfortable with yourself. It involves a willingness to stop running from the pain, and accepting all aspects of who you are during this time. It also means realizing there is a uniqueness to your experience that others may not be able to share in or fully understand.

To reach this point we have to realize that the fear of being alone is much worse than actually being alone. When we experience being alone we discover resources we never knew we had. We also learn to gather the resources we need but don't have. We then are able to accept that aloneness is part of the human condition.

Being alone can become a way of healing ourselves. You need time to be introspective and reflective, to reconnect with disowned thoughts and feelings. Through reclaiming feelings and thoughts you come to realize that you are not empty, but rather full, when alone. This inner fullness comes when you allow yourself to grow and develop, reaching a point of comfort when not in the company of others. Eventually, you will reach the point of understanding that being with another person to escape aloneness is destructive and painful. Learning what you need for healing- so that you can choose to enter into relationships rather than needing one to escape loneliness- is one of your greatest challenges.

Friendship

When we experience pain, especially emotional pain, it is often helpful to share that pain with friends. It is not that they can remedy our pain, but the act of sharing seems to lessen the burden. Unfortunately, many of the friends we had while married will no longer be with us now that we are single. There are three reasons why you may experience the loss of friends. The first is, as a single, you may be seen as a threat to your married friends, as you are now an eligible love-object. If their relationship is not secure, you may pose a threat. It is also threatening to others to acknowledge that one's partner is mortal. Since your partner has died you are a reminder of this fact. Another reason is that since you are now single you have become, regardless of your willingness to accept it, a member of a different subculture— that of being a single adult. It may be more difficult for you to relate to your married friends. If you want to keep your friends you must remember that the similarities of your past are now differences. Other similarities will have to be strengthened. Also, you may want to reach out to others who are in a similar situation, that of being singled again, as they have similar circumstances you can relate to.

Rejection and Guilt

It may not sound rational, but you can feel rejection because you are still alive. We may feel that our spouse chose death, rather than to live with us. This is a normal thought, and part of the grieving process. However, rejection implies there is something wrong with you. You may begin searching for some imagined defect in your personality. What is so terrible about you that your partner would choose death rather than life with you? Perhaps you feel guilty because you did not express your feelings of love often enough. Another cause for guilt is surviving, or moving on with your life. You can feel guilty because you did not want to be left alone; even if it meant your spouse suffered. If your spouse was experiencing pain, you may feel guilty because of your relief from the stress of watching a loved one suffer.

This is not all negative. If, when looking at your own behavior, you find that it causes difficulty in your interactions with others, you can change that. The goal of working through this process is to be able to see yourself as a loving and beautiful person, and to come to appreciate yourself as if you are your own best friend.

Guilt is not entirely useless. It helps us realize we have not lived up to our own standards. However, excessive guilt is destructive. When we live our lives as "ought to's," "should haves," or "could have been," we are not able to live life fully. We end up becoming inhibited and controlled. If you have not lived up to realistic expectations, you may need to make amends (if possible), and change the behavior in the future. If the guilt you feel is based on an unrealistic expectation you need to remind yourself that you did the best with what you had at the time. The goal here is to be able to look rationally at your guilt and see if it is appropriate. To feel guilty because we want to go on with our lives, or that we prayed for the suffering of our loved one to end, is normal. However, to feel guilty because you didn't prevent your spouse's death is being unfair to yourself.

Grief

People experience the stages of grieving in many different ways. However, some patterns do emerge, regardless of whether one is a dumper or dumpee. You will most likely experience denial, bargaining, anger, depression, and eventually acceptance.

Grief is an important part of the healing process once your partner has died. The death of your spouse included a funeral, burial, and the surrounding of friends and relatives. However, the grief process is not something that has a time limit. People, who are well intentioned, will say, "Isn't it time for you to move on with your life? It has been X number of months." What they don't realize is that we need to grieve in order to say good-bye to the relationship and that we have to say good-bye not only to our spouse, but also our way of life. We often limit ourselves by not allowing ourselves to cry and feel the pain. Unfortunately, this only forestalls the grieving process, it doesn't put it aside. We need to acknowledge the pain and the loss of control in our lives. Only then are we able to move on with our lives.

There are two different faces to the bargaining phase of the grief process. For dumpers, it often takes the form of, "Id do anything to prevent this from happening to my love partner." For dumpees, it may mean attending church to guarantee safe passage for your loved one or a willingness to give anything to ensure that the pain will be less. Bargaining can be helpful. Many people come to support groups in an effort to bargain away their grief. In these cases, the person grieving will try to get into another relationship to shortcut the pain and insecurity of being alone. It should be stressed that if you are hurting from a past relationship you will not be able to dedicate the needed time and energy to create an authentic intimate relationship..

The depression stage usually lasts one day longer than we thought we could stand. We spend so much of our energy being concerned with our love partner that when we do not have access to that partner it hurts. You may have the sensation that everything you touch dies. This is not the case, but the feelings of depression still need to be examined and dealt with. Some people argue that depression is anger that has no external outlet. Whatever the cause, it is important to realize that others have, or are experiencing, the same emotion.

When you finally stop asking the question, "Why did my spouse have to die?" the process of acceptance is well underway. The emotional pain of separation does lessen over time. Hopefully, the pain you are experiencing will enable you to learn who you are and to reach out toward a full and enriching experience. Acceptance is funny because we don't know we have it until we are confronted by either our past or someone else's pain. Acceptance can be achieved partially and can slip away when we have uncovered some painful feelings from our past. When acceptance does slip from us it is often an indicator that we are needing more self discovery and personal growth.

Anger

Anger is a natural part of the grieving and therefore, healing, process. You may have many targets for your anger. God is often a good target, because He took your love partner away. You might feel angry with your dead spouse for leaving you, or friends and clergy for not realizing your emotional pain. Even those who understand, or are willing to help, may become targets of your anger. You may also feel angry at yourself because your emotional upheaval makes it difficult to go on with life.

Anger is a feeling, and feelings are a part of life. You may be tempted to deny or suppress your anger. However, anger can be very constructive as a positive energy force because it leads you to acknowledge your humanness and the humanness of others. As you work through your anger you begin to experience feelings of peace, and of letting go of what you could not, and cannot, control.

Letting Go

This difficult and painful process is about releasing our emotional ties with our former spouse. At some point your heart releases all the rights and privileges of being married to your spouse. Your mind declares that it is time to go on with what you still do have, as your focus moves away from what was, toward what can be.

An example of someone who has not disentangled from her past is a widow who still wears her wedding band or refers to herself as Mrs. John Doe, where John is the name of her dead spouse. A part of you may resist the disentanglement process. You may experience anger or guilt as you attempt to let go.

This final stage of the grieving process can be much easier if you have, or develop, other interests such as a job or hobby, and you maintain a good support system. To help you disentangle it is suggested you move the bedroom furniture, put away personal belongings of your dead spouse, and experiment with some small changes in your life. Later, when you have fewer emotional ties to your past you can revisit those items you have put away. However, you may want to have a friend nearby when you journey back into those memories.

Self-Worth

Your self-concept may be at an all-time low when your love-relationship ends. So much of your personality was invested into the relationship it is devastating to face the empty place in your identity. All too often we thought of ourselves only in terms of the relationship. When we used to introduce ourselves to others we often referred to ourselves as the spouse of... When we weren't with our mates others would jokingly ask, "Where's your better half?"

Dr. Fisher found that it's common for people to have a low self image immediately following the loss of a love relationship. He argues that our self image is a learned attitude. The way we refer to ourselves as spouse of, children of, or parents of, gives us a sense of identity. When you are widowed you lose that identification. If your self esteem has dropped, and remains low, the grieving process can become even more difficult.

Transition

You are in the midst of perhaps the greatest transition of your life. What makes it even more difficult is that it wasn't one that you chose. In all aspects of your life you are moving from a lifestyle of marriage toward becoming single.

Beneath this surface transition may be an even larger one - a transition from unconscious influences over your life into a new freedom. With your spouse no longer a part of your life, you may begin to evaluate many of the choices you made in your marriage, including the motivations behind those choices. You may experience a new awareness of how leftovers from your past may be still influencing your life.

Openness

This refers to your willingness to drop your guard, a willingness to pursue intimacy with another person. The thought of becoming vulnerable to another may stir up feelings of fear and guilt. You may have created masks to keep people from knowing your pain in the grieving process. Perhaps you have hid behind masks your entire life. Taking the chance to let someone "in" may seem too risky.

There are many masks you might take on to protect yourself during this time. One common one is the "Merry Widowed." Everything is seen in a positive light, all pain is covered up. Another mask is the "Busy Beaver," which refers to the widowed who preoccupies themselves with only logistical details. This mask means keeping conversations on the surface. There are many different masks. Have you adopted a mask to help cope with the pain and uncertainty of this time?

Masks are not always bad. They are often necessary for surviving difficult circumstances, such as losing a spouse to death. However, there comes a time when the energy required to maintain the mask hinders personal growth and the potential for intimacy. At that point the mask is a burden. You will need to decide when the time is right to begin letting others see beyond your mask. Try writing down the masks you use to protect yourself. Which, if any, developed as a result of your spouse's death? What feelings does each mask hide or protect? Which would you like to let go of?

Love

Typically we define love only in terms of some external object, usually a person. However, the beginning point of true love is with yourself. You may discover some parts of yourself you consider unacceptable; grieving has a way of exposing deeper parts of our being. Learning to embrace those parts is the beginning point of loving others. How can you love others if you don't love yourself?

You have lost the one person toward whom you directed your love. Now you may feel lost trying to direct that same love inward. Perhaps you have not experienced the beauty of that type of acceptance from another person, making it even more difficult to give it to yourself. Yet, this time can become an opportunity to appreciate the unique person you are. In the midst of caring for yourself, you may begin to discover the desire to experience love again with another. You may find it difficult to avoid comparing potential future partners to your former spouse. You may wish to find someone to replace your spouse. While the desire is understandable, it is not possible. However, experiencing intimacy is.

Trust

You may be thinking to yourself, "Don't love others; they can die on you." Then you get past this thought and those who may be available just don't measure up. What's happening is you might be making yourself unavailable so you don't have to be hurt. Being with others requires that we share ourselves. When we trust, we expose ourselves to pain. However, if we don't trust, we merely exist and fail to live life. We lived, our spouses died, and yet if we fail to get involved in life we are the one who is acting emotionally dead. The lack of trust is not necessarily a bad thing, but failure to trust anyone including ourselves, causes pain, doubt, and fear that only we can feel.

Relatedness

As you continue along the "climb," as Dr. Fisher refers to the healing process you are in, you may find others to connect with along the way. It is not uncommon for the widowed to seek out someone else from whom they can receive comfort, support, and encouragement. These "growing" relationships are not necessarily romantic, and often are not permanent.

Sexuality

When you were married you knew what to expect sexually from your love-partner. You may not have always had your needs met or felt satisfied in this area of the relationship, but what you did have was familiar. For some, the thought of entering a sexual relationship may be exciting. For many however, the unknown variables make this stressful.

You are also faced with a new set of choices. What are your values around sex? Losing our love-partner creates the need for sexual fulfillment and exposes the fears we have in becoming intimate with another person. You may even feel guilty for being sexually attracted to someone new.

Singleness

Earlier in the grieving process you may have felt you could not live without another love relationship. When you get to the point of saying, "I am content being single," then you reach a stage of personal satisfaction. This doesn't mean you will be single for the rest of your life, but it does mean you have accepted your aloneness.

If most of your identity revolved around being related to your former spouse, singleness may at first feel like failure. Something inside you may say, "I'm only OK if I'm married." Although this is a difficult belief to change, it is possible for you to renew your view of yourself. This renewal is an awakening, or an understanding that your value as a human being does not come from being related to another person. You are valuable even if you are alone. In your marriage or family of origin you may either have not felt valued, or somehow along the way of bonding, given up your value. Now you have an opportunity to reclaim what is rightfully yours.

Purpose

This exciting time signals that you are nearing the end of the grieving process. You begin to feel alive as if for the first time. You may be opening up to experiences which before were taken for granted or simply neglected, because you were immersed in the pain of losing your spouse.

During this period you stop defining your life in the context of your former marriage. Purpose begins to develop based upon your needs, perceptions, and goals. This may be a time to evaluate the direction your life has been going and decide if its the path you really want. You also begin living more in the present, letting go of the past, while planning ahead for the future.

Freedom

Freedom is about fully being yourself. It is accepting, and acting upon, an integration of your various personality parts. You are free to feel, to think, and to relate. Assuming you are successful in resolving the former building blocks, you are now free to become the person you want to be. You realize that relationships can be your teachers, and that connecting to others means reconnecting with yourself. You have climbed the mountain and are now ready to move on with your life. You have grieved the loss of your former love partner, and are now open to experiencing intimacy with others. Congratulations

This section for the widowed was written and compiled by Nelse Grundvig from Bismark, North Dakota, and Robert Stewart from Denver, Colorado. Thank you Nelse and Robert for an important contribution which allows widowed people to participate and have a more positive experience in the Rebuilding class.

Fisher Widowed and Widowers Adjustment Scale

The following statements are feelings and attitudes that people frequently experience after a love-relationship has ended. Read each statement. Decide how frequently the statement applies to your present feelings and attitudes. Mark your response on your answer sheet. If a statement is not appropriate, try to imagine how you would respond if the statement was appropriate.

The five responses to choose from on the answer sheet are:
> **(1)** almost always   **(2)** usually   **(3)** sometimes   **(4)** seldom   **(5)** almost never

1. I am comfortable telling people my love-partner (spouse) has died.

2. I am physically and emotionally exhausted from morning until night.

3. I am constantly thinking of my former love-partner.

4. I feel rejected by many of the friends I had when I was in the love-relationship.

5. I become upset when I think about my former love-partner.

6. I like being the person I am.

7. I feel like crying because I feel so sad.

8. I can calmly talk to God about being alone.

9. There are many things about my personality I would like to change.

10. It is easy for me to accept my becoming a single person.

11. I feel depressed.

12. I feel emotionally separated from my former love-partner.

13. People would not like me if you got to know me.

14. I feel comfortable visiting my former love-partner's gravesite.

15. I feel like I am an attractive person.

16. I feel as though I am in a daze and the world doesn't seem real.

17. I find myself doing things just because my former love-partner would have liked my doing those things.

18. I feel lonely.

19. There are many things about my body I would like to change.

20. I have many plans and goals for the future.

21. I feel I don't have much sex appeal.

22. I am relating and interacting in many new ways with people since my partner's death.

23. Joining a singles' group would make me feel I was a loser like them.

24. It is easy for me to organize my daily routine of living.

25. I find myself talking about my former love-partner all the time.

26. Because my love-partner is dead, I must not enjoy life.

27. I wish I could unload my feelings of anger and pain on my former love-partner.

28. I feel comfortable being with people.

29. I have trouble concentrating.

30. I think of my former love-partner as a part of me rather than as a separate person.

31. I feel like an okay person.

32. I wish my former love-partner could feel the emotional pain I'm feeling.

33. I have close friends who know and understand me.

34. I am unable to control my emotions.

35. I feel capable of building a deep and meaningful love-relationship.

36. I have trouble sleeping.

37. I easily become angry at my former love-partner.

38. I am afraid to trust people who might become love-partners.

39. Because my love-partner died, I feel I am being punished.

40. I either have no appetite or eat continuously, which is unusual for me..

41. I don't want to accept that my love-partner has died.

42. I force myself to eat even though I'm not hungry.

43. I've decided to join the living; my dead love-partner can no longer satisfy my needs.

44. I feel very frightened inside.

45. It is important that my family, friends, and associates share my feelings about my former love-partner.

46. I feel uncomfortable even thinking about dating.

47. I feel capable of living the kind of life I would like to live.

48. I have noticed my body weight is changing a great deal.

49. I often feel that if I had prayed harder or done things right, my love-partner wouldn't have died.

50. My abdomen feels empty and hollow.

51. I have feelings of romantic love for my deceased love-partner.

52. I can make the decisions I need to because I know and trust my feelings.

53. I sometimes wish my dead partner was alive and I were dead so that he/she could know what it is like to hurt this way.

54. I avoid people even though I want and need friends.

55. I have really made a mess of my life.

56. I sigh a lot.

57. I believe I have accepted the death of my spouse.

58. I perform daily activities in a mechanical and unfeeling manner.

59. I become upset when I think of my dead spouse having a peace I cannot share.

60. I feel capable of dealing with my problems.

61. I blame my former love-partner for dying on me.

62. I am afraid of becoming sexually involved with another person.

63. I feel adequate as a love-partner.

64. I often think about the day I will be able to join my dead partner.

65. I feel detached and removed from activities around me as though I were watching a movie screen.

66. I often imagine having sex with my former love-partner.

67. Life is somehow passing me by.

68. I feel comfortable going by myself to public places such as a movie.

69. It is good to feel alive again after having felt numb and emotionally dead.

70. I feel I know and understand myself.

71. I still feel emotionally committed to my former love-partner.

72. I want to be with people but I feel emotionally distant.

73. I am the type of person I would like to have for a friend.

74. I am afraid of becoming emotionally close to another love-partner.

75. Even on the days when I am feeling good I may suddenly become sad and start crying.

76. I can't believe my partner has died.

77. I become upset when I think my dead partner can no longer share my feelings or my life.

78. I feel I have a normal amount of self-confidence.

79. People seem to enjoy being with me.

80. I feel I can never again give myself permission to be in love.

81. I wake up in the morning feeling there is no good reason for me to get out of bed.

82. I find myself daydreaming about all the good times I had with my love-partner.

83. People want to have a love-relationship with me because I feel like a lovable person.

84. If it were possible, I'd get satisfaction out of letting my dead partner know how much I'm hurting.

85. I feel comfortable going to social events even though I'm single.

86. I feel guilty about my being alive when my love-partner is dead.

87. I feel emotionally insecure.

88. I feel uncomfortable even thinking about having a sexual relationship.

89. I feel emotionally weak and helpless.

90. I think about ending my life with suicide.

91. I no longer feel the need to understand why my partner died.

92. I feel comfortable that my friends know my partner died.

93. I am angry at my former partner because I am left alone.

94. I feel like I am going crazy.

95. I am unable to perform sexually.

96. I feel as though I am the only single person in a couple's society.

97. I feel like a single person rather than a married wo/man.

98. I feel my friends look at me as unstable now that I'm single.

99. I daydream about being with and talking to my former love-partner.

100. I need to improve my feelings of self-worth about being a wo/man.

Note: The scoring results of this questionnaire are not statistically accurate. This scale has not been normed and standardized.

This adjustment Scale for the widowed and widowers was done in part by Nelse Grundvig of Bismark, North Dakota.
Thank you Nelse for an important contribution which allows widowed people to assess their process.

Fisher Widowed and Widowers Adjustment Scale
Answer Sheet

First name   Last name

Address   City   State   Zip

Home phone   Work phone   Date

I am ___ male ___ female.   I am _____ years old   I have been separated _____ months

Who decided to end my relationship? ___ I did ___ my spouse did ___ both of us did ___widowed

Please fill in the following circles to answer the questions on the *Fisher Divorce Adjustment Scale.* The five responses to choose from are:

(1) almost always **(2)** usually **(3)** sometimes **(4)** seldom **(5)** almost never

	1 2 3 4 5		1 2 3 4 5		1 2 3 4 5		1 2 3 4 5
1.	0 0 0 0 0	26.	0 0 0 0 0	51.	0 0 0 0 0	76.	0 0 0 0 0
2.	0 0 0 0 0	27.	0 0 0 0 0	52.	0 0 0 0 0	77.	0 0 0 0 0
3.	0 0 0 0 0	28.	0 0 0 0 0	53.	0 0 0 0 0	78.	0 0 0 0 0
4.	0 0 0 0 0	29.	0 0 0 0 0	54.	0 0 0 0 0	79.	0 0 0 0 0
5.	0 0 0 0 0	30.	0 0 0 0 0	55.	0 0 0 0 0	80.	0 0 0 0 0
6.	0 0 0 0 0	31.	0 0 0 0 0	56.	0 0 0 0 0	81.	0 0 0 0 0
7.	0 0 0 0 0	32.	0 0 0 0 0	57.	0 0 0 0 0	82.	0 0 0 0 0
8.	0 0 0 0 0	33.	0 0 0 0 0	58.	0 0 0 0 0	83.	0 0 0 0 0
9.	0 0 0 0 0	34.	0 0 0 0 0	59.	0 0 0 0 0	84.	0 0 0 0 0
10.	0 0 0 0 0	35.	0 0 0 0 0	60.	0 0 0 0 0	85.	0 0 0 0 0
11.	0 0 0 0 0	36.	0 0 0 0 0	61.	0 0 0 0 0	86.	0 0 0 0 0
12.	0 0 0 0 0	37.	0 0 0 0 0	62.	0 0 0 0 0	87.	0 0 0 0 0
13.	0 0 0 0 0	38.	0 0 0 0 0	63.	0 0 0 0 0	88.	0 0 0 0 0
14.	0 0 0 0 0	39.	0 0 0 0 0	64.	0 0 0 0 0	89.	0 0 0 0 0
15.	0 0 0 0 0	40.	0 0 0 0 0	65.	0 0 0 0 0	90.	0 0 0 0 0
16.	0 0 0 0 0	41.	0 0 0 0 0	66.	0 0 0 0 0	91.	0 0 0 0 0
17.	0 0 0 0 0	42.	0 0 0 0 0	67.	0 0 0 0 0	92.	0 0 0 0 0
18.	0 0 0 0 0	43.	0 0 0 0 0	68.	0 0 0 0 0	93.	0 0 0 0 0
19.	0 0 0 0 0	44.	0 0 0 0 0	69.	0 0 0 0 0	94.	0 0 0 0 0
20.	0 0 0 0 0	45.	0 0 0 0 0	70.	0 0 0 0 0	95.	0 0 0 0 0
21.	0 0 0 0 0	46.	0 0 0 0 0	71.	0 0 0 0 0	96.	0 0 0 0 0
22.	0 0 0 0 0	47.	0 0 0 0 0	72.	0 0 0 0 0	97.	0 0 0 0 0
23.	0 0 0 0 0	48.	0 0 0 0 0	73.	0 0 0 0 0	98.	0 0 0 0 0
24.	0 0 0 0 0	49.	0 0 0 0 0	74.	0 0 0 0 0	99.	0 0 0 0 0
25.	0 0 0 0 0	50.	0 0 0 0 0	75.	0 0 0 0 0	100.	0 0 0 0 0

Note: If you copy this answer sheet on a copy machine, make sure the copy is exactly the same spacing as the original if you want to hand score the answers using the transparencies.

Appendix D
Welcome Volunteer Helpers

You are embarking on one of the most interesting and challenging experiences of your life. Welcome to the team! Your participation in the ten-week Rebuilding seminar has been an important experience, but now you will be involved in a different kind of growth experience. Observing the participants' growth from the perspective of a volunteer helper will be interesting and rewarding.

Hopefully you have learned from the ten-week seminar how to build authentic relationships instead of over/under responsible ones. Now you have a challenge and a test to see if you can be put into a potentially over-responsible position and still remain responsible to yourself. Will you be giving the hungry and hurting people a fish each week or will you be teaching them to fish?

Many of you are extremely motivated to help others as you have been helped but you may be feeling overwhelmed, fearful of hurting others or feeling inadequate as a volunteer. My suggestions are:

- Don't try to walk on water! Be real. Don't be afraid to show your pain. Give examples of how to deal with this pain rather than projecting an image of having worked through everything. The best set of volunteers I ever had in a class had five of the six volunteers ending another love relationship during the ten weeks. They were able to demonstrate to the participants how to make a crisis into a creative experience.

- Remember that active-listening to participants is usually helpful and never harmful. On the other hand, preaching and advice-giving is usually detrimental. The old Indian proverb of trying to understand others by walking a mile in their moccasins before judging them is relevant here. Relax and practice your listening skills and know you can be helpful to others working through the process. After you have learned and practiced these listening skills, use them in all aspects of your life — with friends, children, loved ones, and fellow-workers.

The Rebuilding Seminar is being offered all over North America and in many foreign countries with possibly one half of a million participants by 2000. One of the unique and important features of this model is the volunteer helper support system. Your volunteering makes this model effective in meeting the needs of participants. Thank you for agreeing to share yourself for the next ten weeks.
You will be making a difference in this seminar, in your community, and in the world.

Lovingly,

Bruce

Volunteer Helper Agreement
Fisher Rebuilding Ten Week Educational Seminar

My Duties and Roles as a Volunteer Helper

I understand the duties and role of a volunteer helper in this psycho-educational model are as follows:

- To be supportive and be a good active listener to the seminar participants. I will *not* play the role of a therapist by offering advice, analyzing or diagnosing the participants behavior, or attempting to change their behavior in certain prescribed ways.
- To lead small group discussions with the participants during the weekly seminars.
- To assist the facilitator by keeping attendance, helping with registration, seeing that absent seminar participants receive the handout sheets, organizing activities, and any other such duties as requested by the facilitator.
- To attend at least nine of the ten sessions of the seminar. I will communicate with the facilitator before class time if I will be absent for that session.
- To contribute to the large group discussion of the homework and topic for each session.
- To contact the participants outside of the seminar in order to assist them in doing the homework and learning the material taught in the educational model.

Being a volunteer helper places me in a position of trust. When I am listening to the participant I may hear information of a confidential nature. People who are working through a period of adjustment to a crisis often feel vulnerable, may be looking for answers to relieve their emotional pain, may experience feelings of love for a friendly volunteer helper, and may become angry or emotionally upset at those attempting to help them.

- I will not tell others about the personal information that is shared with me by the participants, other volunteer helpers, or facilitators. I will ask permission from the participant to share important confidential information with the facilitator if I believe the facilitator needs to know. On the other hand, I understand that if a participant is feeling suicidal or threatening to do harm to another I am obligated to share this information with the facilitator or other appropriate helping person(s).
- I agree to *not* become romantically or sexually involved with any participant during the ten week class. I further agree to *not* become romantically or sexually involved after the completion of the class with any former participant who is not legally divorced.
- I will conduct myself in an appropriate manner at all times when acting as a volunteer helper. I agree to *not* become involved in any illegal behavior with the seminar participants while I am a volunteer helper. I understand the facilitator is *not* responsible for any misconduct on my part while I am a volunteer helper.

Termination of My Role as a Volunteer Helper.

I agree to terminate, or be terminated, as a volunteer helper under the following conditions:

- I violate any of the above duties of a volunteer helper.
- I experience emotional burnout resulting in my becoming insensitive to the needs of the participants and not interested in being supportive anymore.
- I become engrossed with my own personal process such as feeling depressed, suicidal, homicidal, or overwhelmed emotionally in such a way that I am not able to be helpful to others.

I understand that I will not receive any financial remuneration for being a volunteer helper. I have read this agreement and understand it completely. I agree to comply with the terms of this agreement and be a volunteer helper during the ten week seminar dates listed below.

_____   _____
Name of Seminar   Dates of Seminar

_____   _____
Volunteer Helper's Signature   Facilitator's Signature

Volunteer Helpers Duties

Congratulations! You have been chosen to be a volunteer helper because you are a *special* person. I challenge you to make this a growing and healing experience for yourself and the participants you are helping. The following is a list of some of your duties.

Before Opening Night
- Convince your hurting friends who are having relationship difficulties to come hear the Rebuilding Block presentation on opening night. It will be helpful to them whether they participate in the class or not.
- Call as many participants that are advance registered for the class as you can. Ask your facilitator for names and phone numbers if you don't have them yet. Those participants receiving calls before opening night really appreciate it.
- Review the Volunteer Helpers Manual. Take the *Fisher Volunteer Assessment Scale* if you haven't already. Read the opening chapters in the textbook. Think about your experience as a participant in the class. How did participating in the class help you in your adjustment process?

Opening Night
This is the most important night for you as a volunteer helper. Do you remember how you felt opening night? Plan to arrive at least fifteen minutes early. Ask your facilitator what you can do to help. Be prepared to talk about one of the Rebuilding Blocks if your facilitator requests it. Here are some rules for opening night:
- Spend as much time as possible talking to people you don't know. Make them feel welcome. Be careful about hugging and spending too much time with your former class mates.
- Anytime during the ten classes, but especially on opening night, make sure if anyone walks out of class that at least one volunteer helper walks out with them. They may want to be alone, but be with them and actively listen to them if possible. Sometimes after talking they may feel strong enough to return to the class.
- Act like the winner that you are! Recently separated people believe that only losers end love relationships. You can help them realize that maybe they are a winner also.
- During break make yourself available to connect with the new participants. See if they have any questions or concerns. Encourage them to register for the class but make sure you give them emotional space to make the decision themselves. They will know when they are ready to participate and trying to pressure them to participate before they are ready will not be beneficial.
- Plan to be available to participants after class. A large percentage of participants will not have found a person they can talk to since the separation. Hearing the Rebuilding Blocks presentation may stimulate a multitude of feelings. I have known participants that talked for several hours after class.
- Determine which participants you are going to call. Work with your facilitator to make sure each participant gets at least two phone calls from volunteers the first week.
- Many times you can start your phone calls to participants immediately after opening night. Most of them will be processing the opening night and not go to sleep for hours after class is over.

Weekly Duties
- Call the facilitator if you are going to be late or absent from class.
- Read the assignments each week and do the homework. You might be surprised at how different the experience is as a volunteer than it was during this class.
- Review your small group questions and be prepared to lead the small group discussion.
- Keep aware of the volunteer duties for yourself and others. Encourage the participants to avoid becoming involved romantically and sexually during the class.
- Keep the phone lines busy with your calls. Alert the facilitator if you are unable to make calls to the participants. Report important feedback that you receive from the participants to your facilitator.
- Keep nurturing yourself. Ask for help and support from other volunteers and the facilitator if you need it. Remember you may be going into a deeper layer in your process than you were able to do when you took the class. It's okay to still be in emotional pain sometimes.

Thank you for your efforts in becoming an effective volunteer helper.   — Bruce

Volunteer Special Assignment Sheet

Opening Night, Date, and Time _____

Name of Seminar _____

Opening Night and Second Night: (Please print your name next to the your assignment)

_____ Bring refreshments to opening night.

_____ Make coffee before and during the meeting. Clean up the coffee pot and refreshment area before we leave.

_____ Help set up chairs and couches before the meeting and put them back the way they were after the meeting.

_____ Put up signs leading from the front door to the room we're meeting in, and take them down afterwards. Also, use the sign-in sheet and transfer all the names and information on it to a current class list by highlighting correct information and adding new names to the class list. Give the class list to the facilitator at the beginning of the break for use during registration.

_____ Greet people at the front door of the building and direct them to the signs leading to the room we're meeting in.

_____ Greet people at the entrance to the room we're meeting in, have them put on name tags using a dark felt pen, and have them sign in on the "Sign-In Sheet." Be sure they have the "Rebuilding Blocks" handout sheet so they can make notes during the presentation.

_____ A male who, when asked to by the facilitator about the benefit you received from the seminar you attended, will share with large group during the presentation.

_____ A female who, when asked to by a facilitator about the benefit you received from the seminar you attended, will share with large group during the presentation.

_____ During registration be in charge of the Class Attendance sheet. Make sure each registered person signs their name and marks the week they would like to have the seminar in their home, and the week they would like to bring refreshments. Make sure someone signs up for week number two for both home and refreshments. Explain what we'll need: the largest room for the big group and as many smaller rooms as possible for small groups. Help arrange for additional chairs when needed. Try and obtain a map to the participant's home at least two weeks in advance so copies can be make and passed out a week ahead of time.

_____ An alternate volunteer who can help other volunteers with their assignments. You'll be the one they call if they are going to miss a class so you can carry out their assignment. Check with the facilitator(s) to see if there's anything special needed that night.

_____ Arrange get-togethers after class and between classes. Start having class parties after the fourth night of class. Be sure to ask only class members to the parties at first. You need to make it as safe as possible for participants.

<u>All volunteer helpers</u> _____ As soon as everything is cleaned up and ready to go after the first session, the volunteers will meet with the facilitator(s) to divide up the class list so that every participant gets a volunteer assigned to call them. This will happen at the meeting location if it can be done before 10:30 PM, otherwise we'll need to meet at a nearby location. See that everyone gets at least one call (two is better) each week for at least the 1st four weeks.

We are really counting on you to be responsible and carry out your assignments!!

Specific Suggestions for Volunteer Helpers

Be friendly, even if the person you talk to seems guarded or short with you. They're probably afraid or mistrusting — its not about you! Be positive and encouraging. Tell them a little about yourself, but be careful not to do all the talking. (see self-disclosure section) If you're comfortable, they'll be more likely to be comfortable too. If you're nervous, they may become a little nervous also. If someone seems anxious, you might say, "Just tell me if you need to go, we can always talk again another time."

Get them talking by asking "open-ended questions," then all you'll need to do is be a good active-listener.

Open-ended Questions. (These are questions that can't be answered "yes" or "no")

How did you hear about the seminar? (If someone referred them, ask, "What did they say about it?")

What do you know about it?

I'd be happy to answer any questions you may have about the seminar.

What's your relationship situation?

What are you hoping to get out of this seminar?

What have you been doing to take care of yourself during this time?

Don't Give Advice!!!

If you need to, you can say: "This is what I (or someone I know) did, and this is how it turned out." Instead of telling them what to do, you can say, "I have felt pretty confused sometimes too, but the answers seem to come to me the more I learn and trust myself to make good decisions." Encourage them to make their own decisions, that will ultimately empower them the most! If you're not sure how to answer a question, say "I don't know, maybe you could ask the facilitator about that." Let them know it's okay if feelings come up for them while they're on the phone, or at any time. Let them feel you don't need to fix it by trying to feel for them, or to diminish their feelings and pain.

Be sure to repeat your name, give them your telephone number, and the best time to reach you at the end of the conversation. Let them know its okay to call you if they have questions or feel like talking. We recommend you call them before opening night. You might say, "Of course I'll be there opening night. I'll be wearing a name tag, so please be sure to come up and say 'hi' to me. Will I see you there?"

Telephone Calls

If you're not in a centered place, don't take or make calls. Take care of yourself. If you get someone very talkative and you need to go, just say, "I've really enjoyed talking with you. I've got some things I need to take care of; hopefully we can connect again soon."

Hello, This is _____ with the Fisher Rebuilding Seminars. The facilitator asked me to give you a call about the upcoming Rebuilding Seminar. Is this a good time to talk?" If yes, "Great!" (If no, "When would be a good time for you?")

"Did you receive the letter we sent you, with directions to the first night? Do you think you'll be able to make it?" (If no, see the "Resistance" section.)

"Were the directions clear about how to get there? I'd like to verify the spelling of your name, your address, and telephone numbers for our class list, would that be all right? This is the information I have (read slowly). Is this all correct? Would you like me to change or add anything?"

Small Groups
- Sit next to the most talkative person.
- Try not to interrupt or cut people off — however sometimes you may need to. Say something like, "I really appreciate your openness, maybe we could talk some more about that at break or during the week. I need to give everyone a chance to share. Who'd like to be next?" (or pick someone). Be sure to follow up one to one!

Come-ons
If someone approaches you to be more than a supportive friend, even if it's asking you to go out after the seminar is over, say something like, "I am really flattered that you like me. I have agreed not to get romantically involved with any of the participants during the 10 weeks. It's nice that you're feeling comfortable enough with me to ask. I want you to stay focused on yourself as much as possible during this time, that's what seems to help people the most. Romantic relationships sometimes have a way of getting in the way of that. You start thinking about the other person all the time instead of working on yourself. Working on yourself is what this seminar is all about."

Resistance Because of Time
"It seemed like a lot of time to me at the beginning, too, but I found that the nights actually went by really fast. I think it was some of the best time I ever spent on myself. I learned a lot and it helped me work through some pretty difficult feelings (or changes). Why don't you just come to the opening night presentation and check it out? It's free and open to the public!"

Resistance Because of Money
"Don't worry about the money. The facilitators know people are often going through money problems at a time like this. He or she will let you work out a payment plan or special arrangements if you need to. Be sure to come opening night, which is free and open to the public. You can talk with the facilitator about your financial concerns at that time."

Fear of Groups and Confidentiality (though they might not bring it up)
"You know everything that's said in these groups is totally confidential, and that includes our telephone conversation, too."

After you have handled basic resistance and they still don't want to come, ask if they'd like to be contacted about future seminars. If they're not interested, be cordial and support them to come sometime in the future. Let the facilitator know they are not interested in coming to the Seminar at this time.

Self-disclosure
"My relationship(or marriage) ended about _____ months/years ago. It was pretty tough, it still hurts sometimes, but things are getting better. Its really working out for the best. I don't mean to say it's been easy, but the group has helped a lot.
"The Rebuilding seminar really helped me:
- I learned a lot about the kinds of things that almost everyone goes through when an important relationship is in trouble or ends.
- I learned a lot about myself too.
- I understand more about my part in the problems in my relationship.
- I found a lot of understanding for the feelings I was having.
- Many people in the seminar were going through the same kinds of things as me.
- I made some good friends I could really talk to, about anything, without worrying about what they'd think of me."

General Guidelines About Volunteering

Make the calls assigned to you. It's easier to make them soon after the meeting night. Make a note on your class list of the people who are in your small group so if they are assigned to you to call, you will remember them. After the third night of class, call the people who were in your small groups, so keep track of participants in your small group on that night. No other calls will be assigned. Encourage participants to call each other. It will help them tremendously, and it will make your life easier too. Carry out your special assignments responsibly. If you are going to miss a class or commitment, contact the "alternate" or another volunteer to handle your responsibility. Be on time if at all possible, especially early on in the seminar, in order to set a good example. Help the facilitator(s) get people back from break as fast as possible when "big group time" is called. Set up carpools with people in your area. Start on opening night when we come back from break by saying, "Everyone from _____ who'd like to carpool, let's meet over there right after class." Have a place in mind to meet, (like a park-n-ride), and be familiar with the directions to get there.

If a participant is really having a hard time, or you are having a problem dealing with them, talk to a facilitator about it right away. Be sensitive to the participants and to each other. If someone is feeling a lot of feelings and needs some extra nurturing, give it to them! If someone doesn't wish to talk in a small group, at break or over the phone, let them gracefully "pass." Be supportive of each other! Talk to another volunteer if you need some support. The more you feel supported, the more you'll be able to support others. Please don't tell participants your problems to the point where they start feeling the urge to take care of you. They need to be focusing on themselves. Sometimes volunteers arrange their schedules so they can get together before or after group to talk about how they're doing, who needs extra support, or check out ideas for outside group gettogethers. It can be very helpful; we strongly recommend it if at all possible.

Make the most of this volunteer opportunity. Just be yourself, because you're the best! That's why you were chosen.

Thank you very much for your help!!

Fisher Volunteer Assessment Scale

This is a self-assessment instrument designed to help evaluate your own readiness to be a volunteer helper. The assessment is divided into various sections to identify the various helping skills better. Please be honest and objective in order to learn as much about yourself as possible. We do not expect you to be perfect. Use your responses as a guideline in your continuing growth process. (Rate yourself on a scale of one to five.)

Active Listening   **Almost Never.... to... Almost Always**

1. I am a good listener.   1 2 3 4 5

2. I concentrate well when I am listening.   1 2 3 4 5

3. I can easily paraphrase in my own words what I heard the helpee say.   1 2 3 4 5

4. I normally maintain eye contact when listening.   1 2 3 4 5

5. My body language indicates to the helpee that I am listening.   1 2 3 4 5

6. My responses indicate that I have been listening.   1 2 3 4 5

7. My responses might be called assertive rather than passive or aggressive.   1 2 3 4 5

8. I respond with "I" messages rather than "you" messages.   1 2 3 4 5

9. I listen rather than give advice.   1 2 3 4 5

10. I believe helpees are capable of solving their problems by talking them out.   1 2 3 4 5

11. I interrupt the helpee only when it is appropriate.   1 2 3 4 5

12. I respond with open-ended questions.   1 2 3 4 5

13. I use helpful active-listening responses.   1 2 3 4 5

14. I do not detract from the helpee's concerns and feelings.   1 2 3 4 5

15. I help the person focus on the main problem and feelings.   1 2 3 4 5

16. I help the person find choices and alternatives without telling them what to do. 1 2 3 4 5

17. I help the person become aware of their own feelings.   1 2 3 4 5

18. I am aware of my judgmental attitudes as they relate to the helpee concerns.   1 2 3 4 5

19. My feedback is descriptive rather than evaluative.   1 2 3 4 5

20. My feedback is specific rather than generalizing.   1 2 3 4 5

21. My feedback meets both my needs and the helpee's needs.   1 2 3 4 5

22. My feedback is directed towards behavior the helpee can change.   1 2 3 4 5

23. My feedback is requested rather than imposed.   1 2 3 4 5

24. My feedback is given as soon as possible after the helpee comments.   1 2 3 4 5

25. I check out my interpretations with the helpee to make sure I am not assuming. 1 2 3 4 5

26. I am comfortable with appropriate silences.   1 2 3 4 5

27. I use physical touching and hugs in an appropriate and helpful manner.   1 2 3 4 5

Barriers to Communication

28. I avoid using generalizing terms like *always* and *never*.　1 2 3 4 5

29. I communicate by using first person pronouns.　1 2 3 4 5

30. I avoid leading questions in order to get the answer I want the helpee to say.　1 2 3 4 5

31. I avoid intellectualizing, non-feeling responses.　1 2 3 4 5

32. The helpee talks more than I do.　1 2 3 4 5

Authentic Rather Than Adaptive/Survivor Active-Listening

33. I build authentic relationships with helpees.　1 2 3 4 5

34. I can choose to use an adaptive part if it is helpful to the helpee.　1 2 3 4 5

35. I avoid over-responsible adaptive rescuing of the helpee.　1 2 3 4 5

36. I understand adaptive behavior can appear to be authentic when it's not.　1 2 3 4 5

37. I am aware which adaptive/survivor part I normally operate from.　1 2 3 4 5

38. I practice self monitoring of my adaptive/survivor parts when active listening.　1 2 3 4 5

39. I can stay in control of my outer critic when active listening.　1 2 3 4 5

40. I am generally aware which adaptive/survivor part the helpee is using.　1 2 3 4 5

41. I am dedicated to continue nurturing myself when working as a volunteer.　1 2 3 4 5

Appropriate Self-Disclosure

42. I can openly share my feelings and experiences with the helpee.　1 2 3 4 5

43. I share my own feelings and experiences in a helpful manner.　1 2 3 4 5

44. I self-disclose only when it is helpful to the helpee.　1 2 3 4 5

45. My self-disclosure aids the helpee in sharing personal feelings and experiences.　1 2 3 4 5

Sensitivity

46. I genuinely care for the helpee.　1 2 3 4 5

47. I can identify and understand the problems and concerns of the helpee.　1 2 3 4 5

48. I can nurture and listen objectively.　1 2 3 4 5

49. My voice tone and language are consistent with those of the helpee.　1 2 3 4 5

50. I am sensitive to what the helpee is "not saying."　1 2 3 4 5

Creativity

51. I am creative in responding to the helpee.   1 2 3 4 5

52. I am creative in finding new ways to active listen that are helpful to the helpee. 1 2 3 4 5

53. I am creative in offering new ideas and attitudes to the helpee.   1 2 3 4 5

54. I am creative in finding new ways of being helpful.   1 2 3 4 5

Emotional Burnout

55. I have trouble concentrating when I am listening to the helpee.   1 2 3 4 5

56. I would rather be doing something other than listening.   1 2 3 4 5

57. I am tired of being around hurting people.   1 2 3 4 5

58. I want to do things for me instead of always helping others.   1 2 3 4 5

59. Helping others is hard work and not enjoyable.   1 2 3 4 5

60. I am listening to avoid feeling rejected or guilty.   1 2 3 4 5

Mechanics

61. I usually arrive at class a few minutes early.   1 2 3 4 5

62. I remain aware of the time when I lead small groups so I can return on time. 1 2 3 4 5

63. I contact my facilitator if I am unable to complete my assigned phone calls. 1 2 3 4 5

64. I am usually available when participants wish to contact me.   1 2 3 4 5

65. I only make commitments when I know I can follow through with them.   1 2 3 4 5

66. I contact my facilitator any time I have doubts or concerns.   1 2 3 4 5

67. I give my facilitator feedback on how I am feeling about my role as volunteer. 1 2 3 4 5

General Rating

68. If I were a helpee, I would want to talk to someone like me.   1 2 3 4 5

69. The participants in my class would rate me as a warm and caring volunteer. 1 2 3 4 5

70. I would rate myself as an effective volunteer helper.   1 2 3 4 5

Books by Dr. Fisher and Colleagues

Rebuilding
When Your Relationship Ends (3rd Edition, 2000)
Bruce Fisher, Ed.D., and Robert E. Alberti, Ph.D.
Softcover: $14.95   304 pages
Popular guide to divorce recovery. The "divorce process rebuilding blocks" format offers a nineteen-step process for putting life back together after divorce. Built on more than two decades of research and practice, *Rebuilding* reflects feedback from, and the experiences of hundreds of thousands of divorced men and women. Clearly the most widely used approach to divorce recovery, Fisher's Rebuilding model has made the divorce process less traumatic, even healthier, for his readers. More than 800,000 in print.

Rebuilding
Audio Version
Bruce Fisher, Ed.D.
Audiocassette: $11.95   90 minutes

Dr. Fisher's warm and personal style guides listeners through the audiotape presentation of the "divorce process rebuilding blocks." The audio version of the bestselling book covers the same model which has aided hundreds of thousands in recovering after ending a love relationship. An invaluable resource, offering listeners caring support and practical guidance. If you like Bruce in print, you'll love him on tape!

Rebuilding Facilitator's Manual
Bruce Fisher, Ed.D., with Jere Bierhaus
Softcover: $50.00   208 pages
This manual is designed to be used with *Rebuilding: When Your Relationship Ends,* and the *Rebuilding Workbook* in leading the "Fisher Rebuilding Ten-Week Educational Seminar." This manual includes everything that is in the *Rebuilding Workbook* plus other material such as the "How to Facilitate" sections and the *Fisher Divorce Adjustment Scale* scoring and research data. It is written to answer any questions leaders might have about facilitating the Seminar.

Loving Choices
An Experience in Growing Relationships (Revised 2nd Edition, 2000)
Bruce Fisher, Ed.D., and Nina Hart
Softcover: $14.95   224 pages
Ever wanted to be better at building or maintaining romantic attachments, friendships, or family connections? Here's help! *Loving Choices* offers a powerful model for communication with yourself and others. Packed with insights, examples, and self-help exercises to help you understand yourself better and develop healing and healthy relationships with the significant others in your life.

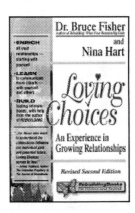

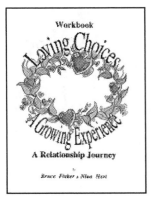

Loving Choices Workbook
A Growing Experience
Bruce Fisher, Ed.D., and Nina Hart
Softcover: $12.00   118 pages
This popular workbook contains practical exercises designed to be used by participants in the Bruce Fisher-Nina Hart twelve-week "Loving Choices" Seminar. It is also helpful for those reading the book, *Loving Choices,* and not participating in the Seminar. Fisher and Hart effectively motivate the reader with journaling, writing reactions and becoming involved with the loving choices process.

Please see following page for more Rebuilding Books

Selected Books in the Rebuilding Books™ Series

Making Intimate Connections
Seven Guidelines for Great Relationships and Better Communication
Albert Ellis, Ph.D., and Ted Crawford
Softcover: $15.95   160 pages

This is the first book to apply Dr. Ellis's famous "Rational Emotive Behavior Therapy" principles to intimate relationships. The seven guidelines for better couple communication offered in this user-friendly guide emphasize non-blaming acceptance, integrity, mutual support, appreciation, replacing irrational ideas and expectations with realistic attitudes.

Getting Apart Together
A Couple's Guide to a Fair Divorce or Separation
Martin Kranitz, M.A.
Softcover: $14.95   208 pages

Guess which couple got more of what they wanted: Charles and Charlotte, who worked out a negotiated settlement together? Or John and Joyce, who let the court settle their differences? Couples who want to negotiate their own divorce settlement now have a comprehensive self-help guide, complete with ground rules, agendas for discussion, sample forms, and options for divorce mediation without "bloodshed."

Parenting After Divorce
A Guide to Resolving Conflicts and Meeting Your Children's Needs
Philip M. Stahl, Ph.D.
Softcover: $15.95   192 pages

Here at last is a realistic perspective on divorce and its effects on children. Featuring knowledgeable advice from an expert custody evaluator, packed with real-world examples, this book avoids idealistic assumptions, and offers practical help for divorcing parents, custody evaluators, family court counselors, marriage and family therapists, and others interested in the well-being of children.

The Divorce Helpbook for Teens
Cynthia MacGregor
Softcover: $13.95   144 pages

Special book for teenagers in divorced and divorcing families. Friendly guide offers a helping hand to teens struggling to answer the tough questions when their parents divorce: Why do parents get divorced? How will the divorce change our lives? Who can I talk to about my problems? What's going to happen next? How do you say "no" to parents who want you to carry messages to, or spy on, the other parent? What is there to talk about when you visit a parent who's moved away?

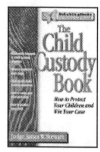

The Child Custody Book
How to Protect Your Children and Win Your Case
Judge James W. Stewart
Softcover: $16.95   176 pages

"It is almost always in your children's best interest to settle a case — with or without mediation — rather than to litigate in court," according to Judge Stewart. His book fully, clearly, and concisely explains the process of court child custody litigation. It shows how custody decisions are made, what can be expected at each stage of the process and how parents can insure that their abilities are clearly presented to persons with influence over the custody decision.

The Divorce Helpbook for Kids
Cynthia MacGregor
Softcover: $12.95   144 pages

Down-to-earth guide addressing many topics troubling kids when their parents divorce: reasons parents get divorced, ways the divorce will change kids' lives; kids' feelings about divorce, things kids can do to help them feel better (and reassurance that they are not to blame); who to talk to; and what's likely to happen next; life after divorce, visitation, custody, straddling two households, and making it all work.

Ask your local or online bookseller, or call 1-800-246-7228 to order direct

Impact ✸ Publishers®
POST OFFICE BOX 6016 • ATASCADERO, CALIFORNIA 93423-6016
Visit us on the Internet at www.impactpublishers.com • Write for our free catalog
Prices effective May 1, 2004 and subject to change without notice.